CALLED T

Geoffrey Chapman Pastoral Studies Series

Making RCIA work, handling the management of change and loss, parish evangelization, diocesan renewal, moral theology at the end of the twentieth century, the challenges raised by *Christifideles Laici*, reconciliation, these are all issues to be covered in the Geoffrey Chapman Pastoral Studies series.

For the clergy, pastoral workers and interested lay people, the series is based on experience, and provides a comprehensive introduction to the issues involved.

The authors are recognized authorities on their subjects and bring their considerable experience and expertise to bear on the series.

ALREADY PUBLISHED IN THE SERIES:

CALLED TO MISSION

*A Workbook for
the Decade of Evangelization*

CHRISTINE DODD

GEOFFREY
CHAPMAN

Geoffrey Chapman
An imprint of Cassell Publishers Limited
Villiers House, 41/47 Strand, London WC2N 5JE, England

First published 1991

British Library Cataloguing in Publication Data
Dodd, Christine
Called to mission.
1. Evangelism
I. Title
269.2

ISBN 0–225–66609–X

Typeset by Intype, London
Printed and bound in Great Britain by
Biddles Ltd, Guildford and King's Lynn

CONTENTS

ACKNOWLEDGEMENTS

In the first instance I am grateful to the following authors and/or publishers for permission to reprint their material (with varying degrees of adaptation).

Texas Bishops, *Pastoral Letter on Evangelization*, April 1989 (reproduced in *Origins*).

Anne Bishop and Eldon Hay, *Telling my Story, Sharing my Faith* (United Church of Canada – Division of Mission).

Cardinal Carlo Maria Martini of Milan, *Let us go to Capernaum*, Symposium of European Bishops, October 1989 (published in *Briefing*, 8 December 1989).

Sharing Our Faith, Telling the Story: A Mission Starter Pack for the Local Church (Board of Mission and Unity, Church of England).

This is the Laity: A Simplification of Christifideles Laici. Used by permission of A. P. Watt Ltd on behalf of the Grail, England.

Pope Paul VI, *Evangelii Nuntiandi* (Catholic Truth Society).

Tim Mayfield, *Thank God for That!* (The Bible Reading Fellowship).

John J. Vincent, *Situation Analysis* (Sheffield: Urban Theology Unit).

Archbishop Patrick Flores, 'The Laity as Agents of Evangelization' (published in *Origins*).

Gordon and Graham Jones, *What I've Always Wanted to Say . . . but never had the courage* (Church Pastoral Aid Society).

Christine Dodd, *Making Scripture Work* (Geoffrey Chapman).

Evangelization Checklist (Office for Evangelization)

All Scripture references except for p. 62 are from the *New Jerusalem Bible*, published and copyright 1985 by Darton, Longman & Todd and Doubleday, a division of Bantam Doubleday Dell Publishing Group, Inc., and used by permission of the publishers.

Every effort has been made to trace copyright holders and we hope no copyright has been infringed. Pardon is sought and apology made if we have overlooked a copyright and a correction will be made in any reprint of this book.

I would also like to record my thanks to all those who have made this book possible. My particular thanks go to Anne King at Geoffrey Chapman who helped shape the book into its final form as well as seeing it through the stages of its publication.

Christine Dodd

INTRODUCTION

It was Sunday morning and she was sitting in her usual place in St Edwin's church. As she looked around her it suddenly dawned on Elizabeth just how many people had smiled at her that morning; just how many people she knew and just how different they all were. In front of her sat the Wilsons. Elizabeth had always thought that David was one of the most gentle and thoughtful people she had ever known. Well-read and articulate, he never seemed to give the slightest hint that his knowledge was greater than that of almost everybody else in the church that day. What always struck Elizabeth was that his humility was real because he didn't think he was being humble. There was something about him which she could only describe as a Christlike attitude. Sarah, his wife, had that open-heartedness which meant that the house was always bursting at the seams with people who had just 'popped in' for a chat or had been brought along by one of the three Wilson children, all of whom had now grown up and were busily engaged in building their own lives. Thomas had recently married and was living in London. Rachel was 19 and about to go off to spend a year with a religious community. (David said that, despite the punk hairstyle, he wouldn't be at all surprised if she didn't end up staying there.) Anne was doing A levels and was hoping to get good enough results next year to study psychology at university. 'They are such naturally good people', thought Elizabeth, 'their faith shines through them.'

Looking to her left she saw Laura. They had often spent long hours together over cups of coffee discussing Laura's growing business. She seemed to have more work than she could handle and had often spoken to Elizabeth about the balance between work and leisure. There could be no doubt about Laura's ability and her business acumen. A leading light in the local Chamber of Commerce, she was becoming more and more immersed in the world of industry. Often she would talk about the problems and the joys which faced her as a Christian in a commercial environment.

Graham had the opposite difficulty. An unemployed steel-worker, he had to struggle, both to make ends meet financially and to keep his own sense of self-worth. Elizabeth was amazed at his apparently unflagging energy for the work he did with the local pastoral care group. If anyone was in trouble with blocked drains, leaking pipes or cars that wouldn't start it was always Graham they turned to, and he always responded with a generosity which seemed unbounded. It was in practical ways that he lived out his faith.

A giggle from behind reminded Elizabeth of the Davies family. Colin had become a full member of the church last Easter and now he, his wife and their four little girls took up the whole pew behind Elizabeth. They had a delightful spontaneity about their faith which she found wistfully attractive. It seemed so fresh and alive for them. One only had to look to see that it meant something special to the whole family.

On the opposite side of the aisle sat Richard. A quiet young man rather prone to bouts of depression, Richard had that marvellous ability to sit and listen for hours and hours to someone else's troubles, often hearing the same story over and over again. He was so shy and self-effacing that often he was overlooked. Elizabeth made a mental note to remind herself to make a point of speaking to him after the service. Yet, she reflected, it was Richard's quietness that often drew people to him. His willingness to listen and not to judge or push his own ideas forward was the very thing which other people found so helpful. It was as if God was listening through him.

'So many people', thought Elizabeth, 'with so much to give.' They had so much goodness about them and a range of gifts which covered just about every need. But, although Elizabeth could see all this in others, when it came to looking at herself it was a different story. It seemed to her that talents and attractive personalities always belonged to others. Of course, had Elizabeth heard what her friends and acquaintances thought about her, she would have discovered that they saw in her gifts she failed to recognize in herself. Her knack of saying the right thing at the right time, her willingness to see the best in people and her sense of humour all made an impression on people. The trouble was she didn't know it. She just thought of herself as bumbling along. She didn't see that she too could be an instrument that God could use: a channel which could spread his love.

There were many people in St Edwin's that morning as there are in churches up and down the country. People who are, in themselves, a treasure-trove of talent and experience and gifts.

In St Edwin's, as in every church, the sheer variety of the people there was one of its strengths. It had so much going for it and yet, how many people inside the church recognized the gifts they had and how these could be used to spread a little of the light of Christ to others? And how many outside the church that morning knew about the Lord that was being proclaimed? Did the people of St Edwin's know the responsibility they had to share their faith? And, even if they did, could they discover the confidence they needed to do it? Could they find the necessary ways and means which would enable others to set out on the journey of faith?

It is to local Christian communities such as St Edwin's that this book is addressed. It is designed to help churches explore in practical ways what they mean by evangelization and what they can do about it. It must be stressed that this book is not a blueprint. It is not a programme for evangelization nor will it solve all problems. It can never be a programme or 'course' because no two local churches have the same needs. Any reader will soon notice that the book is designed to help people work around the subject *for themselves* and not to provide ready-made answers. A few pointers about how to use the book should therefore be mentioned.

How to use this book

1. Each of the chapters in this book is divided into a number of sections exploring the basic ideas in theory, illustrated with examples of 'real life' situations. At the end of each section is suggested group work on the theme. The book can therefore be used as a basis for a small group to think around the whole subject of evangelization in the local church.
2. The exercises can be used consecutively or in isolation. Chapter 7 contains some additional suggestions for group work.
3. Questions for reflection are asked throughout the book to help focus the thoughts of the individuals and groups on what has been said.
4. If you are using the book with a group it is important to ensure that you work out beforehand how you intend to operate and how you plan to tackle the subject. Will you meet weekly, fortnightly or monthly? For how long? Who will be in your group? Will you have breaks or keep going? Questions such as these demand that the leader has a good

advance knowledge of what is contained in the book and a good knowledge of the people in the group. It is essential that the material is *adapted* to meet the needs of the group. The book is the servant not the master and should be used in the most flexible way possible.

5. At the end of your meetings you should not only have widened your own knowledge but you should also be able to take practical action. Careful note should therefore be kept of the plans made in the relevant exercises.

6. It is vital that the rest of the congregation is kept informed and, if possible, involved in what is going on. Although this book is designed with a small group in mind, evangelization is the task of the whole community, not just of one section of it. Consequently every effort must be made to ensure that the thinking, reflection and action which this book may provoke is not seen as the exclusive activity of one small group. There is no reason why some of the exercises could not be undertaken with a much larger group, or adapted for such use.

This book seeks to tackle two real problems that affect most local churches as far as sharing faith is concerned: lack of confidence by individuals and lack of confidence by local communities. It is a 'what to do, how to do it and where to do it' book designed to inject new confidence, overcome fears and open new doors for both individuals and groups. If it succeeds in enabling even one or two people or churches to grasp a little more of the richness of the faith they hold and the way to share it then it will have accomplished its purpose.

Chapter 1

CALLED BY GOD
The essential elements of evangelization

St Edwin's church is much like hundreds of others. It has the usual mixture of people that one might find anywhere. They have different interests, friends, hobbies, lifestyles, backgrounds and temperaments. They have different expectations, different hopes and dreams and different experiences of the joys and sorrows of life. What binds them together is a common faith and a common belief that there is more to life than appears on the surface. The faith they share is one of hope and promise though they may not always be good at sharing it and at times may have their own doubts. This hope and promise is not something St Edwin's should be keeping to themselves but something they should be sharing around. The problem is that they neither know how to go about it nor are they sure quite whether they are capable of doing so. Some have not even really considered what they have to share or why they should share it. For all sorts of reasons they are unsure about all this mission and evangelization business.

If we are honest most of us are not unlike them. Most of us hover between believing we have something worth sharing and not wanting to share it with others. Most of us find ourselves in the half-in, half-out situation. As individuals we half delight in our faith and want others to share it; yet we are frightened about how to do so in a gentle, relevant and loving way. Half-aware that we have gifts that God could use for the good of others, yet reticent about using them. Half-certain that the call to discipleship involves us in more than a private relationship with God and yet scared stiff about what others will think of us if we open our mouths about our faith. We say we believe that God can do all things and yet deep down we do not wish to run the risk of letting him prove it.

Staying in the shallow end

The local community, too, is equally a half-in, half-out scenario. The uncertainty and insecurity which affect us as individuals affect us as communities too. We know deep down that we should go about proclaiming the Gospel in whatever way seems right, proper and sensitive, and yet so often we live on the surface in our churches, busying ourselves with peripheral things. We say we believe that God can and does work through his Church and will guide and give us all we need, but as Peter Marshall once said, 'In too many cases Christians are like deep-sea divers, encased in suits designed for many fathoms deep, bravely marching to pull out plugs in bath tubs.' We have all we need to enable us to swim free yet we are afraid to let go and get out of our depth.

These, often unspoken, yet real fears on the part of both individuals and communities as far as faith sharing is concerned, provoke in us a number of reactions. One reaction is to produce a sense of hopelessness: the task seems so huge.

We are not ready

Another reaction is to try and escape from the uncertainty we feel by proclaiming that we are not ready yet and that, before we can move out into new areas of faith sharing, we must get our own house in order. There is, of course, some truth in this. We do sometimes need to give people encouragement first but we also need to recognize that confidence often comes with the doing of a task. There is also the need to ensure that our communities are ready to receive newcomers and are themselves signs of the Kingdom, but the fact remains that too often we make this 'not ready yet' reaction an excuse for doing little or nothing.

'Kidology'

A third reaction is what might be called the 'kidology' syndrome. This is where we try to convince ourselves that what we are already doing is the best thing since sliced bread and the perfect way to share faith. The fact that nobody is responding is not our fault! We try to convince ourselves that our church doors are always open and that the blame for the fact that no one new is attracted to our community lies with them not with us.

Making space for new members

There are other reactions too. Guilt, powerlessness, an unwillingness to accept change both in ourselves or in our communities can all be discerned. So too can the desire to keep things as they are and not to have to cope with the difficulties which accepting new people may entail. An unwillingness to give up positions of responsibility in the community to newcomers and to accept new ideas all conspire to hold back the task we know is ours. So what are we to do?

This book is about the 'how' of evangelization but it must be said at the start that the 'how' can only make sense if we understand the 'why' of evangelization. We need solid foundations; so we need to look at the essential 'building blocks' which are the basis for all that follows. The first area is summed up in the question 'What is evangelization?'. The second area looks at the basis of our evangelization and the third at the essential elements for it. Unless we examine these first, using all the practical suggestions and ideas which follow, we will be building a house of bricks on sand. We need good foundations and solid blocks on which to construct our activities. Let us then look carefully at our three foundation stones.

What is evangelization?

Mission, evangelization, witness and proclamation are a complex of words that often fill us with foreboding. To many of us these words conjure up pictures or methods of making the Good News known with which we do not feel comfortable. For some that unease centres around the notion of evangelization as big rallies and direct proclamation in mass groups. For some the unease is a fear of making the Good News known in a direct form to those individuals with whom we come into contact. For others still the fear is that evangelization is remote or divorced from social action and justice. Whatever form our unease takes it is important that we seriously address the question 'What is evangelization?'.

> The word evangelization . . . means literally 'communication of the Gospel', the spreading of the Good News of Jesus Christ. Its root word the Greek *evangelion*, means simply 'good news'.
> (Texas Bishops, *Pastoral Letter on Evangelization*)

This immediately points out one very important factor: evangelization is not only conversion. It is not method. It is not technique. It is not a programme. It is a mentality and an attitude. There is no *one* right way of doing evangelization. It is the proclaiming of the Good News, however that is undertaken. That proclamation must also take into account the corporate nature of our lives. We belong to one another, we develop relationships with one another. If evangelization is about discovering a living relationship with Christ, it is also about a relationship with the other members of his Body, the Church.

What we do, what we say and who we are

Evangelization then is a much broader term than we often imagine. For this reason there can be no divide between social justice and care for the poor and the physical needs of men and women, and direct proclamation by word. As we shall see, word and deed go together. Both are important elements within the overall task. So, when the people of St Edwin's set up a Drop-In Centre for the large number of elderly people that live within their local area they are engaged in the work of evangelization. They are proclaiming by what they do God's love, care and concern for these people. But St Edwin's also has the task of answering the questions of these people if they should ask why they do what they do. It must not just be all social work nor must it be all word.

If evangelization therefore is the broad term meaning the proclamation of the Good News both by what we do and what we say, it is also the term for proclaiming the Good News by who we are. A life that is truly compassionate, caring and Christlike speaks volumes about what makes that person tick. Our words will mean nothing unless they are backed up by a life that shows the truth of those words. This applies to communities as well as to individuals. What we are dealing with in this book then is the whole life of a local church community: its actions, its words and its very being. Evangelization is, or should be, the motivation behind its existence.

Group work on the theme: What is evangelization?

Step 1
In this first meeting we shall start by getting to know one another if we do not already do so. (Try to find some other way of doing

this than 'the names around the circle' method.) For instance, ask people to say one thing about themselves which will help people remember who they are, e.g. 'My name is Richard. I'm a football referee.'

Begin by asking God to direct your thoughts and plans.

Step 2
Here are some definitions of evangelization. Read them through carefully. Evangelization is:

> Talking to others about my faith and answering questions, when asked.
> Living a Christian life.
> Taking care of others.
> Giving to the poor.
> Making Christ known in my local community.
> Challenging the systems that oppress people.
> Standing for justice.
> Being involved in organizations and groups that care for others.
> Taking part in rallies.
> Sharing the story of what God has done for me.

There is truth in all of these statements. List any others you would want to add. Discuss them in the group.

Step 3
Produce a definition of evangelization for your local church. 'For [insert name of your church] church evangelization is . . .'

Step 4
Make sure you keep this definition in sight during all the sessions that follow. You may want to amend or alter it as you go along but it is important not to lose sight of what evangelization means to your church community.

Step 5
Close with a time of prayer asking God to help you in the task he has given you.

The basis of our evangelization

The next question we must ask is 'What is the basis for our evangelization?' It is not enough to know what we are doing, we must also know *why* we are doing it. Why does St Edwin's run its Drop-In Centre in the way it does? Why does this aspect of its evangelization take this particular form? We should expect to find all forms of evangelization based on at least three key beliefs.

1. The first is a recognition that our evangelization is based upon God himself. The Good News comes from God and is not something we have dreamed up for ourselves. The Gospel we are sent to proclaim is not 'our' Gospel. It is God's Glad Tidings. As such it finds its start and its finish in him. If, therefore, we secretly or overtly proclaim the Good News to make us feel good or to indulge in some sort of 'head count' or to fill the seats in our churches because this is the sign of a successful Christian community, then we must question our motives. The Gospel is not something we possess to keep it to ourselves. It is something we share with others and sharing means giving away. Because the Gospel is from God we are the instruments through which he shares, through which he gives away his Good News. We cannot lay claim to it as our own secret, private and personal possession.

2. The second basis on which our evangelization is to be built concerns the *contents* of the Good News. Here we are at the heart of the matter. The Good News is based on God. The message not only comes from him, it is about him and primarily it is a message of God's involvement with us in the world that he has created. The depths of that involvement can be seen in the coming, the life, the death and the resurrection of Jesus. Here is God immersed in human history and in human lives; a message for all time of God's concern both for the individual and for the whole of the creation which is his. Thus the Good News is not just about the Jesus of history. It is about the Jesus of now; the Jesus who is alive and present with his people in the here and now. This message is one we hear so often that we can become blind to its greatness. The basis of our evangelization is a living, present Christ who can and does affect the lives of individuals and communities. If we truly believe this message and glimpse, however imperfectly, its greatness, evangelization becomes inevitable. If you have something wonderful you wish to share it and if you have been given a beautiful present beyond price you wish others to know of the richness of the giver. That is why at the centre of all evangelization must lie a living relationship with God. Without this we are but 'a gong booming or a cymbal clashing' (1 Corinthians 13:1).

3. The third basis for all our evangelization is that this Good News is not restricted to certain people or certain groups. The Good News is for *all*, regardless of race, colour, age, sex or status. God's care and love is for all and the Good News, the Gospel, is for all. This means that we cannot and must not make the reception of the proclamation of the Gospel into a sort of obstacle course for people to overcome. It demands that the local Christian community finds ways and means of spreading the message in a variety of ways to a variety of people. No one way is going to be right for everybody and no one group has a monopoly on the Gospel.

Group work on the theme:
The basis of our evangelization

You will need copies of old magazines and newspapers (local and national).

Step 1
We begin by getting to know something new about each other. This is important as this is only the second meeting. Each person has a piece of paper. Write your name at the top and underneath write three things about yourself that others might not know. 'Invisible' things will be better than the obvious, e.g. 'I enjoy drawing' is better than 'I am a woman'.

Step 2
Find someone in the group you do not know well. Exchange your sentences.

Step 3
In a moment of silent prayer thank God for each other.

Step 4

Ask the group to look through the newspapers and magazines for good news.
(a) List what makes for 'good news'.
(b) How is God at work in the stories?
(c) Who is involved in the stories? What does this have to say about the basis of our evangelization?

Step 5 Reflection

Thank God for the way he works in his world. Ask him to help you see the Good News in your life and the lives around you.

Step 1 adapted from Anne Bishop and Eldon Hay, *Telling my Story, sharing my Faith* (Division of Mission in Canada, The United Church of Canada).

The essential elements of our evangelization

'What shall we do?' and 'How shall we do it?' are the two questions most local churches commonly ask with regard to evangelization. In St Edwin's a small group of people got together to discuss these very questions but it soon became apparent that they needed first to think about the basic principles on which their actions were to be built. There are at least four essential elements to all evangelization: service, proclamation, celebration and dignity.

1. Service

We have already noted that the proclamation of the Word cannot be divorced from service to individuals and community. The life of Jesus was one of deeds as well as words. His proclamation of the Good News of God's love was seen in action as well as declared in speech.

> Evangelization cannot just mean proclaiming the Word from the height of the pulpit. It means that before anything else we should be 'a gospel' ourselves in deed and word.
>
> (Cardinal Martini of Milan, *Let us go to Capernaum*)

This evangelization by service to the community and to individual members within it will be carried out in different ways in different local churches but whatever is done, and however it is done, it constitutes evangelization. The Word is already proclaimed whenever we serve others.

Question: How do we see our activities as vehicles through which the Good News is shared with others?

Question: What distinction do we make (if any) between evangelization through word and deed? Do we give greater emphasis to one rather than the other? Should we?

2. Proclaiming the Word

We have noted that the Word is already truly proclaimed in service. Through our action it finds expression but we must turn now to the explicit proclamation of the Gospel. Here we need to notice two important points. First, the Gospel does demand that we speak out. It demands that we find ways of expressing in words our resistance to everything which damages people and prevents them from living fully human lives. Christ came that we might have fullness of life and anything which prevents that or opposes it demands our attention. So proclaiming the Word has a prophetic element to it. We do not speak the Good News into a vacuum. We must take into account the real situations in which people live and its demand to put oneself 'on the line'.

This prophetic element of proclaiming the Good News can be seen in the example of Maria. Maria belonged to St Martin's church. She lived about half a mile away and from her window she looked out at a home for elderly people. It was a beautiful new complex with all the residents could wish for in the way of amenities. It had been opened a year before and the residents were now part of the street's community. Maria noticed however that very few of them went to church. One day she was having a leisurely chat with Arthur. 'The problem is', he said, 'the bus stop is in the wrong place. If they would only re-route it up and around this street instead of stopping it down at the bottom of the hill we could all get out and about more.' 'Why don't you see the powers that be?' asked Maria. 'Oh, believe me, we've tried but we seem to get nowhere.'

Maria was now undecided about whether or not to do what her conscience told her to do. In the end she decided that she must do something so, taking a day off work, she presented herself at the offices of the local bus company. She got no joy. Next she wrote — still nothing. A petition from the residents and other local people didn't seem to be doing much although Maria thought she noticed a slight weakening in the last letter

she received: 'The matter would be re-considered.' Months
went by and Maria's enquiries were met by the all too familiar
brick wall. Eventually she contacted the local paper and the
local radio station, who featured what had now become a major
local issue. It took Maria and a small group of people from her
church 18 months to get the bus re-routed but she and her
supporters did it in the end. Now the residents have a fuller
life, and they have access to the world outside their front doors.
It has not however made much difference to the number of
those who come to church. 'Why did you do it?' asked Arthur
one day. 'Because it was right to do it and because it would be
hypocritical of us to sit in our church on Sunday and proclaim
that God cares for you and not allow him to use us to show
you that he cares for you', replied Maria.

(Adapted from *Sharing our Faith, Telling the Story: A Mission Starter
Pack for the Local Church*. Board for Mission and Unity of the Church
of England.)

This story is a wonderful example of a combination of evangelization as action and as word. The Word is proclaimed in a
direct way through Maria's confrontation with the bus company
which prevented the residents of the home from living a fuller
and more complete life. It is also proclaimed in her closing
words to Arthur.

The second important point about the direct proclamation
of the Word concerns a willingness to proclaim openly that
everything good and true and which helps human beings to
live a more fulfilled life is considered by us to be a gift from
God. So part of proclaiming the Gospel is to encourage and
support the goodness that we find in our society. It is to proclaim that that which is constructive and enhances human
potential is part of God's work in his world. So, when the local
newspaper published a superb article on the work of the local
hospice for the dying, the people of Newtown Way church
wrote to the editor not only to congratulate him but to put on
record their thanks to the staff of the hospice for 'enabling
people to die with that dignity which God wishes for all people'.
The local paper published the letter. It led to quite a correspon-
dence through the columns of the paper about death and about
the ultimate purpose in life.

This proclaiming the Word by both challenging all that is
harmful and praising all that is good, must, of course, have its
explicit elements. We should not be afraid to mention God or

to proclaim that the goodness is his doing. Nor should we be afraid to answer directly those who question us and require us to give an account of ourselves and of the faith in which we believe. This, of course, is not always easy. Most of us are quite cowardly when it comes to speaking about our faith. We prefer to hope that our faith will shine forth in what we do but that we will not be challenged about it. George is a good example. He is a machine operator at a local factory which makes parts for refrigerators. It is Monday morning and pouring with rain as it has done all weekend. George's fellow workers are discussing what sort of a weekend they have had. It is Tony who turns to George and asks what he did yesterday. 'Much the same as usual', replies George. 'Which is?' George hesitates. Should he tell Tony that yesterday morning, as usual, he went to church? He is tempted to keep quiet, not because he fears what Tony will think but because he is afraid that his relationship with Tony will alter. He has been getting on fine with the lad and has been able to witness by the sort of person that he is. All that may change if Tony misunderstands. George decides that he must say something. 'Went to church Sunday morning as usual', he says as matter-of-factly as possible, 'Took the kids to see Grandma in the afternoon.' Tony said nothing. It was only when his sister was seriously injured in a car crash about six months later that George noticed that Tony was turning to him, not just for support, but with all sorts of questions about life and death and about how to cope.

(Adapted from *Sharing our Faith, Telling the Story*.)

Question: How can we explicitly praise all that is good in the society around us and point to the God who is behind and within it?

Question: In what ways should we be challenging all that prevents the Good News from being a reality in people's lives?

3. Celebration

The third essential element in our evangelization should be celebration. If the Word which we proclaim is truly good and if we are to proclaim that goodness then the celebration of it is vitally important. To this should be added an awareness of the fact that there are specific times in everyone's life when celebrations are vitally important.

Baptisms, weddings and anniversary celebrations which take place within the church community setting should be real celebrations.

'It is not enough to require as a condition for baptism a strong and explicit faith on the part of those asking for baptism, if we do not at the same time require a similar commitment from the community.'

(Cardinal Martini, *Let us go to Capernaum*)

The commitment from the community must take the form of a real and living celebration of the entry of this human being into the Christian community. In addition:

The meeting with parents who request baptism for their child should take place in such a way that it becomes an opportunity for them to experience the Good News of the unconditional love God has for them.

(Cardinal Martini, *Let us go to Capernaum*)

This means that those who wish to celebrate with us special moments in their lives must find within our communities something which proclaims the Good News to them, in other words a real celebration of God's love.

Question: In what ways are our celebrations worthy of the name? What is lacking?

Question: In what ways could we enhance the rites that mark our journey through life (baptisms, weddings, funerals) so that they become real celebrations and thus vehicles of the Good News of God's love?

4. Dignity

The final essential element in all evangelization within the local church community must be the hallmark of dignity. Evangelization in whatever form it takes must never ride roughshod over people. If it does this it will, of course, not be Good News for them at all! Evangelization must be done with respect, with gentleness and with understanding of those to whom we proclaim. This approach does not mean any weakening of the Gospel on our part. It is doing what Christ did: to receive people with dignity and to proclaim the Gospel, the Good News, to them with respect. Our *methods* of proclaiming the Good News must reflect this Christlike attitude. If they do not do so, not only will people fail to listen to us but they could well be given a completely wrong image of the God that we proclaim. Even in situations of confrontation when we speak out to oppose all that is harmful to the growth and potential of human beings, we must not seek to destroy the perpetrators. Condemning the sin is very different from condemning the sinner. The aim must be not only to release those who are oppressed and unable to hear the Good News but also to release the oppressor. The dignity of a human being is a God given and a very precious thing. It must never be destroyed. Being aware of this precious dignity should prevent us from saying or doing anything which is likely to knock down rather than build up. It should act as a check on us and encourage us to listen as well as speak so that our speaking may be relevant and in tune with what God is already doing in people.

Question: What must we guard against in our evangelization?

Question: How could our local community help others know they are of value to God and to others?

Group work on the theme:
The essential elements of evangelization

Step 1
Begin the meeting with a time of prayer.

Step 2
Find one story from the group which illustrates an experience that you know of where evangelization was carried out through:
Service to others
Proclamation of the direct Word
Celebration
Enhancing dignity.

Step 3
Read Luke 18:35–43.

Step 4
Compare your stories with the Gospel story. In what ways do they link up? How did Jesus proclaim the Good News through each of the four elements?

Step 5

In the light of your discussion how are you going to spread what you have learned about these four elements to others in your church community? (Be specific and make sure you do it at some stage.)

Step 6

Close with a time of reflection.

Chapter 2

CALLED TO HOLINESS
A holy community

Introduction

I suspect that many of us, as we look back on the way in which we ourselves have been evangelized, will discover that people have been the main instruments God has used in the process. If we look closely we will often find that, even in those areas where we think God has spoken 'directly', people have been involved. For instance, we know that God speaks through Scripture. But Scripture itself is the story of God's involvement with people and Scripture itself was recorded by people for people. Often, too, Scripture is interpreted for us by men and women in a whole variety of ways.

So then, people are at the core of evangelization. Essentially it is not about techniques or programmes or methods. Evangelization is a people-process. It is about women and men. It is very important to grasp this fact right at the start because it is so easy for a local church to become immersed in the 'how' of evangelization and to get bogged down in the question of methods and techniques. As we shall see, these are important but they are only the means to the end and, in any case, it needs people to put them into practice. Our first and greatest resource is not the many programmes which are available to us, it is the people who make up our communities.

If we can see that people are more important than programmes then we must seriously consider the potential that lies within our own local communities and parishes. We must ask the question — what is the primary requirement which will enable any Christian to let their 'light shine in people's sight, so that, seeing your good works, they may give praise to your Father in heaven' (Matthew 5:16)? There is one essential prerequisite. It is the call, the privilege and the responsibility of every Christian, namely, the call to holiness. It is this, above all, which will act as our primary and most important resource to enable others to discover the fullness of life Jesus promised.

The call of holiness

When I look back over my own life it has not been the people who have been the most 'successful' or the most efficient or the most talented who have been the greater force for my evangelization. It has been the people whose relationship with God has been the most transparent. In other words, it has been the holiest people. These men and women would not call themselves holy. They certainly were, and are, not perfect. But holiness, like evangelization, is a process, a road along which we are walking. Some have walked further along the road than others, some have a very close relationship with God that spills over and can be seen by those whose lives they influence and touch. Holiness is to do with being transformed so that we have the mind and the attitude of Christ. It is about the process of becoming more Christlike, and that call is to all of us. It is not just for pastors, nuns or priests. In the document *Christifideles Laici* Pope John Paul II reminds us of this very forcibly.

> The primary vocation of the laity is to become holy people. This is true of every member of the Church without exception. This vocation is an absolute essential.
>
> (*Christifideles Laici*, 23)

Stephen was an example of a holy person. He worked in a local insurance office. In one sense there was nothing very extraordinary about him at all. He led an ordinary sort of life, was married with three children. Yet there was about Stephen a deep inner tranquillity and a sense of completeness or wholeness which marked him out. It was not that Stephen did not suffer from times of depression, confusion or sadness. Yet despite that, indeed sometimes because of it, Stephen's awareness of a God who was real and living for him shone through. His patience, care and non-judgemental attitude were clear for all to see.

A misunderstanding

When it comes to the question of becoming the holy people we are called to be, with its consequent power for evangelization, we discover a very real difficulty. Most of us fail to see that we are capable of holiness and fail to see that such holiness is possible for us. This difficulty often occurs because we have the wrong expectations of what this call to holiness means. We are not called to have the same sort of spirituality as an enclosed religious. We need to find the path to holiness which is right for us. A lot of thought has recently been given to the need for real lay spirituality and about the diversity of ways in which lay people in particular are called to be holy people in the world. We need to take on board the fact that we *are* called, and that it is possible for us to respond. We will begin to do this when we see that there is no 'right way'. God leads us all on different paths to holiness. I pray differently from you. You pray differently from me. No one way is better than another. You pray as only you can pray. No one can do it like you because your relationship with God is unique.

Life in the world

What links you and me and every other Christian together on the path to holiness is that our praying is done in a very busy life which is largely lived in a secular world. We need to take this on board and to realize that for us holiness, coming closer to God, finding, listening and responding to God is done in and through the secular world. This is very important as far as evangelization is concerned because it means that our prayer and the world in which we evangelize are intimately linked with each other. Our spirituality should take its character from the circumstances of our life. It should not be a separate activity in which we try to forget everything. Rather, in our prayer, in our search for holiness, we take to God the world in which we live, and we find God in the world in which we live. For us there can be no secular/sacred divide.

Called to be where we are

This awareness that our prayer and our call to holiness is to be exercised in the world should have a 'knock-on-effect' as far as our call to evangelization is concerned. It should, and can, release us from a great deal of tension. It means that in our prayer we do not have to strive to wipe out the traces of the world. Rather it enables us to pray in, with and through the world in which we live. God needs us to pray where we are in the midst of our secular society because that *is* where we live and because he only has us to do it. We are thus called, not to escape from the world but to transform it.

The laity do not live two parallel lives; one spiritual life with its own demands, one secular life with the demands of home, work, and the world around them. In God's plan, every area of life without exception is meant to reveal Christ's love. Every activity and situation, every responsibility, offers occasions for glorifying God and serving others.

(*Christifideles Laici*, 59)

This lay holiness to which we are called must express itself in involvement in our world. Our spirituality must have something to do with sanctifying the world. True lay spirituality must give us the strength and guidance and closeness to Christ that we need to have in order to share in his mission.

Here is an exercise to help the group explore their own call to holiness.

Group work on the theme: The call to holiness

Step 1   What is holiness?
On a large piece of paper write down as many definitions of holiness as the group can think of. Ask people to shout the definition out without any discussion as to what they mean. When you have all the definitions on the sheet discuss which of them seems to best express what the group thinks holiness means.

Step 2
In pairs ask people to share their own experience of meeting holy people in the light of their definitions. In particular, ask them to think about how these people acted as evangelizers for them. What was it about them that proclaimed the Gospel?

Step 3
In the whole group invite any sharing of these experiences that participants may wish to make.

Step 4
Read the following passage:

> Father
> I want those you have given me
> to be with me where I am,
> so that they may always see my glory
> which you have given me

because you loved me
before the foundation of the world.
Father, Upright One,
the world has not known you,
but I have known you,
and these have known
that you have sent me.
I have made your name known to them
and will continue to make it known,
so that the love with which you loved me
may be in them,
and so that I may be in them.

(John 17:24–26)

Allow a few moments of silence for participants to reflect on the passage.

Jesus prays that his followers may be with him where he is. What do you think this means in your own daily life?

Jesus prays that the love with which the Father loves him may be in us. What does this mean for evangelization?

Step 5
Ask people to reflect between now and the next session on the question: How does God call me to holiness?

Becoming holy

If we take the call to holiness seriously and see a holy life as a primary instrument of evangelization then the question arises: How can we grow in holiness? How can we become holy; a holiness which will be a powerful message to others of our commitment to Christ? What we shall do here is to look at three essential elements in how we respond to the call to holiness, all of which have an effect on the evangelization process.

The first essential is a *willingness to open our eyes* and really look at what God is doing all around us. The call to holiness does not mean withdrawal into some fantasy world in which there is only 'me and God'. The call to holiness is the call to see, listen and respond to God as he makes himself known to us. This making himself known is done in many different ways. To step out on the path towards the fullness of life Christ promised means opening our eyes to see where he is leading us and to see where he can be discovered. Our difficulty is that so often we fail to see him. He is there before our very eyes in the people around us, in the world he has made and in the opportunities he has given us but we fail to recognize him. This 'seeing Christ all around us' has an important part to play in our evangelization, as we shall see later on. It is important because it means we do not so much take Christ to people as help them to discover where he already is.

The second essential is a *willingness to open our ears*. We need to do this in two ways. First of all we need to open our ears to what God is saying to us and secondly we need to open our ears to what others are saying to us. Often, of course, God will be speaking through other people and just as we fail to see him in others, so we often fail to hear him in others. Becoming holy means a willingness to listen, to listen to God and to listen to each other. Only if we listen to both will our evangelization be relevant and only if we listen to both will the work of Christ in us be brought to fruition.

Having looked and listened, the third essential is a *willingness to respond*. We shall get nowhere on the path to holiness if we fail to make a response to the Christ who is calling us through what we see and hear. Now, this responding happens in many different ways, but it must affect us at two levels. Interiorly, we must allow God to work away in us to transform us. Outwardly, the call to holiness must issue in service to others. We respond to God as we respond to others. As we meet their needs, hear their problems, support, encourage or are simply there, then we are responding to God. It is as we respond to him in these ways that we also evangelize those around us. It is really a case of being aware that we cannot ask others to respond if we do not respond ourselves. We need to respond both in allowing ourselves to be open to God and in allowing him to use us.

Discovering the God who is amongst us and responding to him with the greatest faith and trust we can muster is no easy task. It demands single-mindedness; it demands commitment and it demands time. Yet there is no escape from this primary necessity for holiness of life if our evangelization is to be true to the Gospel. We cannot be preaching one thing and living another.

Group work on the theme:
Becoming holy

Step 1
Read the following passage:

> Jesus also said, 'This is what the kingdom of God is like. A man scatters seed on the land. Night and day, while he sleeps, when he is awake, the seed is sprouting and growing; how, he does not know. Of its own accord the land produces first the shoot, then the ear, then the full grain in the ear. And when the crop is ready, at once he starts to reap because the harvest has come.'
>
> (Mark 4:26–29)

In the light of the passage discuss what, in your own life, helps you grow in holiness.

Discuss what hinders you.

Step 2
Read the following:

> The bodies of Richard Johnson (aged 9) and his elder sister Rachel (aged 13) were discovered at Newham-on-Sea yesterday morning. Richard, a strong swimmer for his age, was swept out to sea when he got into difficulties while bathing. His elder sister, also a good swimmer, had gone to his rescue but both were unable to cope with the strong cross-currents which are notorious in that part of Newham bay.
>
> Eye-witnesses said that the alarm was raised immediately it was realized that Richard was in trouble but that Rachel had gone to his rescue and both were carried out to sea before the in-shore rescue boat could reach them. The local coastguard said, 'It was a tremendous act of heroism on Rachel's part to try and save her brother. Only a few minutes more and we would have been able to save them both.' A relative of the family told the *Newham News*, 'The family is devastated, Richard and Rachel were the apple of their parents' eyes. Our whole world has fallen apart.'

Step 3
Discuss in the group what questions of faith does a passage like this raise for us? Where is God to be seen in this situation? What is he saying to us? What response does he ask of us? Can you see any way in which responding to a situation like this helps us to grow in holiness?

Holiness for the world

As we have seen, the call to holiness and our response to that call takes place within the world in which we live. That world, as we know, is torn apart by violence, hatred, greed and suffering. In our own society it is also a world where the acquisition of material possessions plays an important part in the lives of many people. The secular world of Europe and North America has not, however, blotted out the questions that have been asked for generations. The search for meaning, for a purpose in life and for the 'other dimension' are as real now as they ever were. Questions about these things are asked by many people who would not see themselves as religious in any way. This search for meaning sometimes leads to an exploration which can take the traveller down many avenues. It also leads people to take seriously those whom they see as having grasped something of that 'other dimension' in their own lives; that is, people who have begun to walk the path of holiness to a greater or lesser degree. We need to look at this much more closely because here a real meeting-point is provided between God and those who are searching for him. In other words, the process of evangelization can and should happen at this point and it can and should happen in the most natural way possible.

People are still searching

It is very easy to overlook the fact that the search and the longing for the transcendent is very real today and that this has never been blotted out by our secular world. The desire to find some way of fulfilling that longing manifests itself in many different ways, from interest in yoga or transcendental meditation to involvement in astrology. We need to realize, too, that people discover an 'otherness' in what we might term 'non-religious' ways. Let me give an example. Not long ago I went to a concert. I was sitting in one of the cheaper seats and couldn't see the orchestra but I could see part of the audience. As the concert progressed and as people became immersed in the music it was very clear that for many of them this was indeed a very spiritual experience. The music was reaching parts of them that other activities could not reach. It was touching something in them that was not touched during most of their everyday situations. For many it was an awareness of an 'other dimension'. They might not have used the word 'spiritual' to describe what was happening to them, indeed they might have found it difficult to describe it at all but, nonetheless, it was providing a deep inner experience. For some people this happens through music, for others it may happen through art or through physical movement or through creative activities. As we shall see in the next section it is important that our local communities take seriously this other dimension that is the experience of many people. The search and longing for something other, something beyond us, for transcendence which is felt by so many people, provides us with glorious opportunities for evangelization.

People also look for clues to the other dimension in the lives of those around them. When they come across someone whom they see as having grasped even a little of a reality that they themselves long for, someone who is grappling with the questions of meaning in life, their own inner longings are thrown into sharp relief. When they come across someone who really seems to have 'got it all together' then that person can appear extremely attractive. The best examples of this in our modern-day society are people like Mother Teresa, Desmond Tutu and Oscar Romero. These people evangelize by being who they are as well as by what they do. Now, I am well aware that most of us will not become Desmond Tutus or Mother Teresas or Oscar Romeros but nonetheless the same principle applies. The combination of the call of Christ to holiness and the holiness that issues in a life given to others which these people exemplify, should characterize our own lives. It will, perhaps, surprise us to discover just how one or two steps along the road towards holiness lived in the world can influence others. A friend of mine, who would claim no religious affiliation whatsoever and indeed would say that he is an agnostic, has been extremely impressed by a mutual acquaintance because every time he meets her she never says a bad word about anyone. The fact that she behaves this way because she has a deep inner awareness that God loves each and every person is just beginning to rub off on my friend.

God is there already

This need to see the longing for transcendence and otherness in the people around us has a profound impact on the way in which we evangelize. It means that we must realize that in the world in which we live God is already at work. It means that we must realize that people do have an experience of him even if they may not put his name to it or call it religious. That means that in our call to holiness, in keeping our ears and our eyes open we must be able and willing to see where he is already at work and to enter into dialogue with him. It means that when we begin the processes of evangelization we must be willing to respond to the transcendent that is already in people and to realize that the transcendent in us can be a profound instrument for God to use. It is with these two cardinal points in mind that we will now turn to thoughts about the local community as a holy people and its role in evangelization.

Group work on the theme: Holiness for the world

Step 1
Think of a 'secular' incident in your life which meant a lot to you. (It may be an experience of beauty or joy or sadness.) What was the event? What did you experience? What did you discover?

Step 2
Share with others in the group as much or as little as you wish of this incident.

Step 3
Discuss: How do you think non-religious people express a longing for a transcendent element in their lives today?

Step 4
Share how you think our call to holiness relates to their longings.

Step 5
Reflect for a while in silence about the steps you as an individual should make in response to what you have learnt.

Step 6
Read the following together as a closing prayer.

And Mary said:
My soul proclaims the greatness of the Lord
and my spirit rejoices in God my Saviour;
because he has looked upon the humiliation of his servant.

Yes, from now onwards all generations will call me blessed,
for the Almighty has done great things for me.
Holy is his name,
and his faithful love extends age after age to those who fear
    him.
He has used the power of his arm,
he has routed the arrogant of heart.
He has pulled down princes from their thrones and raised high
    the lowly.
He has filled the starving with good things, sent the rich away
    empty.
He has come to the help of Israel his servant, mindful of his
    faithful love
— according to the promise he made to our ancestors—
of his mercy to Abraham and to his descendents for ever.

(Luke 1:46–55)

A holy community

In the light of this need to experience something of the beyond,
the other, how should the local church community respond?
We need to offer opportunities for people to explore this dimension of their lives. It seems to me that there are four areas which
any local church might consider as a means of responding to
this situation.

1. A chance to explore

One of these four areas is *providing space*. If people are to explore
the 'other' dimension of their lives they must have the space in
which to do so. Helen is a married woman with two teenage
children. As well as looking after her home she has a part-time
job which she enjoys very much. She gets great satisfaction out
of both aspects of her life, her job and her family. She is a busy
person but no more so than most of us. Yet Helen feels that
there is something missing in her life. She finds it difficult to
articulate it or to put her finger on it but she just feels that she
would like to be able to explore a different dimension of herself.
She sometimes feels she is living only on the surface of life and
that, no matter how much fulfilment she gets from her family
and job, she has not yet explored her own inner self. In order
to do this she needs time, she needs the right atmosphere, she

needs to talk things over with people, and she needs to be given a number of different examples and experiences in order to try things out for herself. She needs to be able to listen to how other people have found their own inner self. And she needs to find ways of giving herself permission and time to explore this other side of herself.

The Church should be providing ways and means for this. It should provide people with various opportunities to explore this other dimension that they have within them. It should also provide them with the appropriate flexibility and freedom in which to discover themselves. On the whole the Church is very bad at this. We clutter up our corporate life with a great many 'things'. Our communities are full of organizations, activities and events and, as we shall see, these are an important and invaluable tool in our evangelistic task. However, alongside all this activity we need to provide room in which people can explore that 'other' side. Of all communities the Church should be the one where this can happen. It is, after all, concerned with God and therefore should be offering the opportunities for people to search for meaning and discover how God can be relevant in their own lives.

2. Exploring in other directions

The second area we need to look at is linked with the provision of this 'space'. Our local churches should be providing a chance for women and men to *explore the riches and treasures of Christian spirituality*. The search for the transcendent and for a relevant 'otherness' may lead people into many different areas. Peter has been through a whole range of experiences in his search. He has been to India looking at Eastern religions, he has tried yoga and he has looked at some of the world's major religions. People will try out and explore many different forms of spirituality within the course of their search. They will also test one form against another. They may search among the mystics of the East or on the psychiatrist's couch of the West, or in any one of a dozen different ways. But what do they meet when they come searching within the Christian tradition? Does the local church offer them a chance to explore Christian spirituality in a context and a way which they find both relevant and fulfilling? Once again we are not always very good at providing this. The immense riches and treasures of our Christian spiritual tradition lie hidden and buried, and those searching for them never have a chance to see them in all their beauty. This living heritage which is a pearl of great price remains buried in the ground. It is not unearthed because so many do not know it is even there.

3. A chance to celebrate

The third area which requires our consideration is that of *celebration*. Often people become aware of the desire to search for meaning at specific and important times in their lives. Times of sorrow or pain often raise questions for people. What is it all about? Why does a God of love allow so much suffering? Is the time between my birth and my death all there is to existence? Is the material and physical the only dimension to reality? Times of joy and happiness can also raise questions which express this search for meaning and 'otherness'. Can a world so full of beauty have been created by chance? What is the source of the love I feel for another person? What accounts for the joy I experience in listening to music or seeing a beautiful scene or a work of art? And why do I experience such a sense of wonder at seeing new life and new growth?

The Church has always offered people a chance to celebrate those moments in their lives which are of supreme happiness or desperate sadness for them; baptisms, weddings and funerals are the most obvious. We saw in Chapter 1 the importance of the idea of celebration. But should the Church not also be offering opportunities for people to celebrate other moments of joy and pain in their lives, moments in which the search for the transcendent is often crystallized?

When baby David came along it was not only his parents, Alan and Maria, who were delighted. It was the whole family of grandparents, aunts and uncles. For the grandparents this was their first grandchild. It was the first nephew for Maria's brothers and sisters. It was a cause of immense celebration and the whole family wanted the baptism of baby David to be a way of expressing their joy that this new life had come into the world. Maria and Alan and their family were lucky. Their local Christian community had thought through how it could best celebrate this time of joy with new parents, but it is not always the case. Too often our churches do not really offer the chance for people to celebrate in the way that they might. Baptism offers one opportunity for the Church to celebrate along with people. There are many others. Celebration does not happen in a vacuum. It happens when people come together. Therefore the Church cannot simply offer a chance for others to celebrate. Such activity only becomes meaningful when the community celebrates alongside them and with them.

4. A chance to understand

At the same time as celebrating with people, the Church should be enabling them to *explore the questions* which these celebrations are about. Once again, we are not very good at this. The longing people have to mark these moments in their lives is clear, for they still come to us even though their link with us may be quite tenuous. Somehow our life as a local church community and their lives touch and yet they never really meet. It is as if we are travelling along parallel lines shouting at each other across the void and communicating with each other on one level and yet somehow never truly 'getting it together'. There may be any number of reasons for this. We may not be hearing the questions they are really asking. We may be using the wrong language. There may be a difference in expectations. They may not be able to articulate just why they have come at all. All this, and so much more, prevents us from sharing with them in these important moments in their lives. As we saw in Chapter 1, celebration is one of the key factors in relevant evangelization. We saw there too that this was more than just church services or liturgy. Nevertheless, the way our worship is conducted is an essential element in our evangelization. Those who come to us infrequently to celebrate the important moments on their life journey must therefore experience two things. They must experience the celebrating community that is there to enter with them into the joy or the pain of their experience, and they must find a means of expressing that experience which speaks for them to and about the transcendent. This raises the whole question of what we do about our contact with those who come only occasionally, whether it be for a baptism, or for their child's First Communion or Confirmation, or for a marriage or a funeral. There is no one answer to all this. Each local church community must work out and discuss for itself what the celebration part of evangelization means in their own situation and how that celebration is to be carried out with, for and involving those who come into contact with us.

Offering space, a chance to explore the Christian tradition

and celebrations which are relevant to those we meet are not enough in themselves. If any local church community is to faithfully proclaim the Gospel, this spirituality element, this awareness of the transcendent, must spill over into *love and service for others*.

5. A chance to serve

Angela went to church every Sunday. She had a rich life of prayer, though she herself may not always have thought this. But Angela had her feet well and truly on the ground. When she looked at the Jesus of the gospels as she did most days she was confronted by his attitude to other people, and confronted by her own unwillingness to treat people in the same way. It was a Saturday morning when she saw the elderly lady who lived opposite her struggling with a pair of shears to cut the hedge that surrounded her front garden. Angela was shortly on her way out to do her shopping. She had a busy day ahead including a meeting at the church that afternoon. She hadn't the time or the inclination to stop and to help Mrs Powers. Besides, she had yet to fit in the few moments that she spent in prayer each day. And so she left the window and sat down, opening the gospels as she usually did. The Jesus she read about was one who 'cured many who were sick with diseases of one kind or another' (Mark 1:34). It struck her then that it was impossible for her to leave Mrs Powers struggling with her hedge while she herself got on with her prayers, especially as she was praying to that same Jesus who spent his time in love and service for others. She ended up going across the road with her own electric hedge-cutter to give Mrs Powers a hand.

This evangelization through love and service is essential, we cannot become an 'other worldly' community. The story of the Incarnation will not allow us to do this. Jesus came and was totally immersed in a real, painful and disturbed world. The fact that he spent his life in, and indeed died for, love of others will not allow us to become anything other than as immersed as he was in a world full of violence and terror as well as full of joy. His Incarnation means that we cannot avoid involvement with the world and retreat into some sort of 'transcendent ghetto'. The 'other' element in our community life, as well as in our individual life, is of enormous importance but we must not use it as an excuse to evade contact with an immersion in the reality of daily living. We need the horizontal as well as the vertical dimension to our corporate life. If we do not have both, then our evangelization is not being true to the Gospel. It is not being true to the Jesus who proclaimed the Kingdom of God but who also lived, died and rose again to bring that Kingdom into the reality of everyday situations.

Group work on the theme:
A holy community

We have seen that there are at least four ways in which the local church can offer opportunities for people to explore the transcendent dimension of their lives. It can do this by:

(a) providing opportunities for people to find space in their lives;
(b) providing opportunities for people to explore the riches of Christian spirituality;
(c) providing opportunities for people to celebrate the goodness in their lives;
(d) providing opportunities for love and service of others.

In order to look at how each of these works in our local churches, here are four simple exercises. If you have time you may like to do all four in one session. However, it is probably better to spread them out and do them separately.

A. PROVIDING OPPORTUNITIES FOR PEOPLE TO FIND SPACE IN THEIR LIVES

Step 1

Discuss your own experience of needing space to be yourself.
   How do you find such space in your life?
   What do you need?

Step 2

In the course of their journey he came to a village, and a woman named Martha welcomed him into her house. She had a sister called Mary, who sat down at the Lord's feet and listened to him speaking. Now Martha, who was distracted with all the serving, came to him and said, 'Lord, do you not care that my sister is leaving me to do the serving all by myself? Please tell her to help me.' But the Lord answered, 'Martha, Martha,' he said, 'you worry and fret about so many things and yet few are needed, indeed only one. It is Mary who has chosen the better part, and it is not to be taken from her.'

(Luke 10:38–42)

Who are you most like in the story? Why?
What do you think is the relationship between activity and personal space? (Discuss this in relation to your own life and the life of your church community.)

Step 3
How does your church offer different opportunities for people to find their own personal space?
What more could you do (be practical and realistic)?

B. PROVIDING OPPORTUNITIES FOR PEOPLE TO EXPLORE THE RICHNESS OF OUR CHRISTIAN HERITAGE

Step 1
In pairs spend a few moments talking about your own experience of Christian spirituality. What do you find most helpful? What do you find least helpful?

Step 2
Here is a short meditation which uses the imagination and silence. It is one form of spirituality. Try it and see how you get on.

Someone in the group slowly reads the following passage:

> Imagine yourself sitting by a river. It is a pleasant summery day. You can hear the wind in the trees and see the grass on the bank swaying in the breeze. You can hear the sound of the water as it bubbles over the rocks. The sunlight glitters on the running stream. As you sit there listening and looking you notice a figure walking towards you. He smiles. It is Jesus. He sits down beside you. He asks what you are thinking about. What do you say to him? What does he say to you?

Stay silent for as long as seems right.

Step 3
In pairs discuss your experience of what has just happened.

Step 4
In the group talk about whether you found the exercise helpful or not. If it was helpful, why? If not, why not?

Did you find the period of silence a good experience or difficult to cope with?

Step 5
How does your church offer different opportunities for people to experience the diversity and richness of Christian spirituality? What more could you do?

C. PROVIDING OPPORTUNITIES FOR CELEBRATION

Step 1
On a large sheet of paper list the different celebrations that take place in your local church (e.g. baptisms, weddings, confirmations, anniversaries etc.).

Step 2
For each of these events estimate the number of people who come into contact with your church community. What is your total?

Step 3
Try to estimate how many of these people are:

- closely connected with your church
- loosely connected with your church
- not really connected at all with your church.

Step 4
In the light of your findings try to answer the following questions:

(a) *Who* in your church meets these people (apart from the priest or minister)?
(b) In *what* ways is the contact of your church with these people enabling them to experience a real celebration?
(c) *How* does your church welcome them?
(d) *How* (if at all) does your church celebrate with them?
(e) *What* more could you do or what changes could you make?
(f) In *what* other ways could you help people to celebrate the important moments of their lives?

D. PROVIDING OPPORTUNITIES FOR SERVICE

Step 1
List all the different activities that take place in your church. All aspects of your community life should be included: worship, social life and pastoral care.

Step 2
Using your list place the activities on the following diagram, putting
them in the appropriate section. (Some may belong to both.)

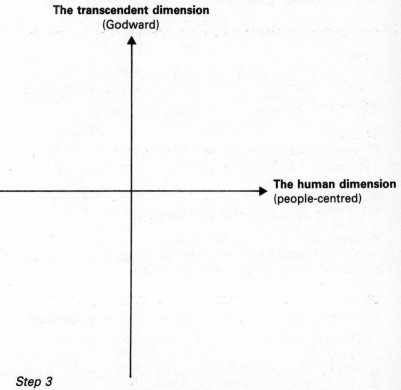

The transcendent dimension
(Godward)

The human dimension
(people-centred)

Step 3
Ask yourselves:

- Is the transcendent dimension emphasized at the expense of
  the caring and social side of your community?
- Is the social and caring side emphasized at the expense of the
  transcendent?
- How do the two interrelate in your local church?
- How does the call to be a holy Christian community spill over
  into the call to love and serve others?

Chapter 3

CALLED TO PILGRIMAGE
The journey of faith

We saw in the last chapter how the call to holiness is a primary one in our task of evangelization. This process of conforming ourselves to the likeness of Christ so that others may see him within us and within our communities is not accomplished overnight. It takes time, and moving towards its fulfilment is rather like being on a journey or a pilgrimage. When we go on holiday or move from one place to another we almost always come back home having visited new places or having discovered new things, however small those discoveries may be. Our journey has changed us. We are not quite the same as before. Perhaps we are more open to new ideas as we have met and talked to new people, or perhaps we are more aware of ourselves as we have coped with new situations. This theme of journey or pilgrimage is a common one in the Scriptures. It is also a common one in the history and tradition of the Church which, in the words of Vatican II, sees itself as 'the pilgrim people of God'. In our task of evangelization this theme of pilgrimage is an important one to consider both as it relates to ourselves and as it relates to those to whom we witness. The first area we must look at in this context is that of a personal pilgrimage. Unless we see ourselves being on a journey towards Christlikeness with all that entails in terms of stops and starts, disappointments and failures, exploration and discovery, our evangelization will be impoverished.

Our personal journey

When Joan looked at the photograph she was amazed. It had been taken fifteen years before but she was astonished to see how much she had changed. Physically, she had aged on her journey through life. Over the years her body had changed. All of us make a physical journey from our birth to our death. Like Joan our bodies change as we grow and then age. In the psychological sense we also make a journey as we learn to cope with the ups and downs of life. The things that happen to us, the joys and sorrows that we experience, force us to react and reflect. From each of these experiences we learn.

We make a journey too in the spiritual sense. If we are serious about our faith, the things that happen to us and the way we reflect upon those happenings will affect the way we think about our faith. A great deal has been written about the stages of faith and development. Such studies are very helpful but we must treat them with a certain amount of caution for we are all unique individuals and we all grow and develop in different ways and at different speeds. The basic idea of these stages of faith is that we move from the literal faith of childhood in which (if we have been lucky enough to be brought up in a Christian family) we accept the faith of our parents, towards a mature faith which goes on searching for fulfilment. We do this through various stages of questioning and testing and reflecting. Understanding where we are on our own faith journey is important because it enables us to recognize that others are on a journey and that part of the process of sharing faith with them is to walk with them along their path. We can only do this if we realize that we ourselves have not yet reached the goal and that, like them, we are continually being evangelized by those who walk with us.

Mark is a good illustration of this. When he went to visit Mrs Davis the process was a two-way one. Mrs Davis was in her eighties and crippled with arthritis. She was almost completely housebound. Mark was asked to go to visit her by the Pastoral Care Group at his church. Mark himself would say that, at first, his attitude left a lot to be desired. He was going to visit Mrs Davis because she was a poor old lady in need of support. At the same time he would be able to witness to his faith, but his attitude towards her was rather patronizing. He had the faith — she needed it! In reality it turned out very, very differently. Mark soon discovered that Mrs Davis had a far deeper spirituality than he could have imagined. Housebound, she would spend long hours in prayer, and her attitude to Mark was one of welcome and warmth. He soon discovered that it was not a case of him 'taking the Gospel' to Mrs Davis but that very often she was 'taking the Gospel' to him. He was being evangelized by her. She had a wealth of life experience and had come a long way on the journey of faith. She was sharing it with him as much as he was sharing his youth and vitality with her.

Evangelization is not something we do to others as if we have

reached the end of our journey. It is something we do for each other as we all walk the path towards that fullness of life Christ wishes each one of us to have. It is important therefore to reflect on this and to spend some time discovering where we are on our journey and where others interact with it.

Group work on the theme: Our personal journey

Step 1
Spend a few moments asking God to show you how he has been active in your life.

Step 2
Read John 1:43–46.

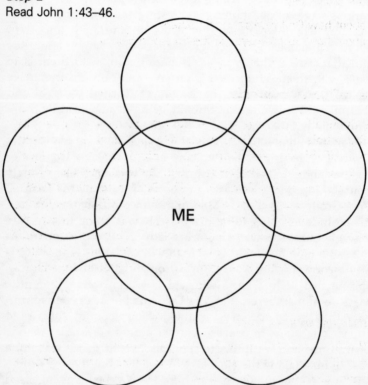

Write in the circles the names of those in whom you have seen God at work and who have influenced your life. You might like to use one circle for every period of your life, e.g. senior school, teenage years, etc.

Step 3
Individually fill in the diagram on p. 40. The aim is to look back over your life in order to see how God has been at work on your journey and how he has worked through others who have been part of your life. (Allow 10 minutes for this.)

Step 4
Come back together and share in groups of four or five something you have discovered about God's activity. Discuss how you have been evangelized by others, i.e. how God has brought you closer to him through other people.

Step 5
In the whole group list any common factors you have discovered in your discussion:

(a) about how God works through others
(b) about how God uses you in the lives of others.

The pilgrim church

The theme of pilgrimage applies not only to the individual but to the whole of Christ's Church. We shall look in the next section of this chapter at the call to pilgrimage for the local church. Here we are concerned with the fact that the whole universal Church is called to be 'The Pilgrim People of God'. This understanding of the whole Church as a pilgrim people is not new but was really brought into prominence by Vatican II. It is important to realize that the universal Church sees herself as a people on the move. The evangelizing task of the whole Church raises a number of important factors which we should explore.

1. Each one of us is called

In the first place this universal pilgrim people is made up of many different parts. In her task of proclaiming the Gospel all her members have a role to play.

All the members of the Church make up the People of God, the Body of Christ. Being a 'member' does not change the fact that each member is unique. Christ's call to go into the vineyard is meant for the Church as a whole, but equally for each individual member. St

Gregory the Great summed up this truth: 'In the Holy Church all are nourished by each one and each one is nourished by all.'

(*Christifideles Laici*, 28)

There can be no doubt about the priority of this task and no excuses for anyone to opt out.

Christ's command to preach the Gospel never loses its force . . . He calls each person by name and no true follower can hold back.

(*Christifideles Laici*, 33)

This means we dare no longer think of ourselves only in a passive role as if the laity's task is only to 'pray, pay and obey'. Every Christian is called to see herself or himself as part of a great company of believers on the move whose task it is to share their faith with others. Everyone, by virtue of their baptism, must share this responsibility and this privilege. How each individual within the body goes about discovering their unique and irreplaceable task and the gifts and talents that they have within them in order to fulfil that task is something we will look at in Chapter 5. Here, the fact that each is called is of paramount importance and demands our attention.

Question: In what ways do you think God has called you as an individual member of the Church to share your faith with others?

Question: In what ways do you 'hold back' from doing so and why?

2. *The Gospel in context*

The next thing we need to note about this pilgrimage of the universal Church is that it does not take place in isolation from the world in which we live. Any journey or pilgrimage takes place in a context. We move on our journey not in a vacuum but within a particular culture and at a particular time. This has important implications for us with regard to our proclamation of the Gospel. It means that we cannot see the Church and the world as travelling along parallel lines so that neither influences nor touches the other. If this were the case the Good News would not be Good News at all because the message would never be able to touch the lives of those around us. No, the Church and the world travel along together; they interrelate. The Church must be immersed and involved in the world in which we live and must journey along with it. The Church has always recognized this and seen the necessity to proclaim the Good News in ways that are relevant to those around her. This means that as we travel along we must listen to the society in which we live and use the language and the images which will make sense in a rapidly changing world.

Such an awareness that the Church and the world are both on the move does *not* mean that the Church changes the Gospel to fit in with society. It *does* mean that the Church changes the way the eternal, unchanging Gospel is presented. There is nothing new in this. As time has progressed and the world has altered, the Church herself has always been on the move in order to present the Good News of Christ in ways that make sense to the society in which she exists. We see an example of this in the recent history of the Church. Recognizing that society had changed and that celebrating the liturgy in Latin was preventing many people from appreciating the richness of the worship of the Church, the Second Vatican Council authorized the use of the vernacular, the ordinary language of the people. Though many thought, and some still think, this should not have been allowed it is nevertheless true that for many people their relationship with God has been given a new lease of life and a new relevance because of the change. The Church, the pilgrim people of God, recognized the world had journeyed on and herself made a move so as to develop ways of enabling people to respond more fully to the eternal Gospel she has always preached.

Question: In what ways do you think society has changed in the last ten years? How has the pilgrim Church responded to those changes?

3. Coping with change

The pilgrim people of God moves in order to try and find new ways of bringing Good News to a rapidly changing world but that inevitably means change. The world in which the Church proclaims the Gospel does not remain static. Neither does the Church. But coping with change can be extremely difficult and sometimes painful. There is no point in changing for change's sake but there is a point in changing if, by that change, the Gospel can be proclaimed more effectively and those around us can come to a greater awareness of the God who is already within them. That the Church has undergone tremendous change on her journey is an undeniable fact. Some of this change has been quite rapid and has taken place in recent times. Some people within this pilgrim people of God have been able to cope with these changes with open arms, seeing within them a chance for new life and growth. Others have grudgingly accepted the changes that have come and some still find coping with a new set of circumstances extremely difficult. Whatever situation we happen to be in we must realize that others are on the journey with us. We are part of the same body that has within it those who want to move along faster than others and those who do not wish to move at all. This inevitably involves a certain amount of tension and sometimes not a little hurt. Those who believe that the Church is moving too slowly become frustrated and sometimes cynical and may even opt out, believing that there is more justice within the world than there is within the Church to which they belong. Those for whom the Church is moving too quickly can become entrenched, seeing any movement on the pilgrimage as a 'watering down' of the faith that the Church proclaims. Yet both these groups are part of the same family.

In one sense, in her evangelistic task, the Church needs both the new and the old. Like the man in the gospel she needs to bring out of her storehouse things old and new. The one needs the other. Those for whom change is very difficult need to see within the other group that faith is possible in a rapidly changing and materialistic world. Those for whom the Church is not moving fast enough need to realize that their brothers and sisters fear that if the Church moves too fast a great deal of value may be lost and the riches of Christian tradition may be discarded without good reason. The first group reminds the second of the roots to which we belong. The second reminds the first that the roots are there to produce growth. These tensions which exist within the universal Church will, as we shall see in the next section, exist within the local church too. In the task of proclaiming the Gospel in the local situation there will be some who will want to move faster than others. There will be those who wish to move outwards and those who think that movement is happening in the wrong direction or that we should not even be moving at all.

Group work on the theme: Coping with change

Step 1
Spend a short time in silence asking God to help you to be honest and open with him and with each other.

Step 2
Read Acts 5:17–42. In this passage there are three main individuals
or groups of people:

- the apostles who preach fearlessly in the Temple.
- the High Priest and the Sanhedrin who demand that they stop.
- Gamaliel who advises the Sanhedrin to free the apostles.

Step 3
Discuss:

- What motivates each of the three?
- Can you see elements of these in your church?
- What does the passage say to our situation about coping with
  change and the tension this involves?

Step 4
Close with a time of prayer asking for God's guidance on the future
life of your church.

4. Beyond the church

The search for faith in which we, as members of the Body of
Christ are engaged, is not confined to the Church. As the pilgrim people of God journey onwards we are surrounded by
others who are also on a journey. Such journeys are not to be
despised. The Church knows that the search for faith happens
in Christians of all traditions, in those of other faiths and in all
those who seek God with sincerity. The searching for truth, the
reverence for nature and the desire to seek for the transcendent
which characterized the life of Hari, a Buddhist, mean that he
has much in common with Christians. We can learn from his
tradition and see something of our own faith reflected in the
teachings and way of life of a different faith.

   This search for God by those who have no close connection
with the Church at all is an important element in our task of
evangelization. The work of God has already begun in people
such as Hari, indeed in many it has progressed a very long
way. We can neither despise not patronize the work that God
is doing within them. Nor should we think that we are taking
Christ to them. He is already among them and working within
them even though they may never mention his name. One of
the tasks of the Church is to enable people to name the God
who is already at work within them. It is to help them see that

they also are on a pilgrimage. Such an attitude of respect and understanding towards those among whom we live makes a very big difference to the way in which we evangelize.

Sammy Philips would not call himself a Christian. He never darkened the doors of any local church. He showed no interest in religion of any sort. Yet when I was walking along a footpath in a National Park with Sammy he suddenly stopped and picked up a leaf which had fallen from a tree. For a while he studied it in silence. Then he turned to me, smiled and in a simple way said, 'I guess there has to be someone who makes everything. If there wasn't how would I know this leaf is as beautiful as it is?' That God was working in Sammy I have no doubt and that Sammy was responding to God, even though he may not have been able to name him, seemed just as clear.

If we look at the gospels we notice that the one thing Jesus always does is to treat people with respect and dignity. He looks for the good within them and he always looks for the way in which his Father is working within those who surround him. He is clear and unambiguous in his proclamation of the Good News but he never despises those with whom he is in contact.

Question: Think of some people you know who are not connected with the Church. Can you see God at work in them? How?

Question: How does your church recognize that people are at different stages on the journey of faith?

5. Evangelization — the task of the church

The final factor that we need to note about the pilgrim people of God is that on this pilgrimage evangelization is essential.

We wish to affirm once more that the task of evangelizing all people constitutes the essential mission of the Church. It is a task and mission which the vast and profound changes of present day society make all the more urgent. Evangelizing is in fact the grace and vocation proper to the Church, her deepest identity. She exists in order to evangelize.

(Pope Paul VI, *Evangelii Nuntiandi*, 14)

Pope Paul VI goes on to talk not only about the vocation of the Church to evangelize, but about the fact that she herself is evangelized. Here we have two sides of a single coin.

The Church is an evangelizer but she begins by being evangelized herself. She is a community of believers, the community of hope, lived and communicated . . . She always needs to be called afresh by him and reunited. In brief, this means that she has a constant need of being evangelized. She wishes to retain freshness, vigour and strength in order to proclaim the Gospel.

(Pope Paul VI, *Evangelii Nuntiandi*, 15)

We see then that one aspect of the Church's task is to evangelize and the other is to be evangelized. To do this the Church acts as a body within which we are the individual members, proclaiming the Gospel to each other as well as to those outside the Church. This means that, to give it a technical term, evangelization is ecclesial. It happens through the Body of Christ, the Church. We do not proclaim our own ideas or our own selves; we act within a local community which is part of a wider and universal family which we call the Church.

> Christianity — in the total, fullest sense — must include Church. For Jesus to reach all strata of humanity, for Jesus to be proclaimed to all the nations and all time he needs his body, the Church. To say that I have accepted Jesus into my heart but have not accepted his body, the Church, is only to accept Jesus in a partial manner.
>
> (Texas Bishops, *Pastoral Letter on Evangelization*)

This idea of being part of a worldwide body can have a marked effect on people. When James became a committed Christian many of his friends were puzzled that every Sunday he went off to his local church. It was Bill who remarked that he could understand what James had done because he could see that the Church had some people within it who were prepared to stand up for what they believed. 'I cannot say I know why they do it', said Bill, 'I can't for the life of me think why Oscar Romero put himself at risk as he did but I admire him for doing it and what he believed in must be pretty powerful stuff if it meant he was willing to die for it.' So, when we invite people to put their trust in Jesus, we also invite them to become part of his body, the Church. That means, of course, that the Church must be the sort of community which proclaims by its very life a Christlike attitude.

Question: Do you agree with the quote from the Texas Bishops? Why or why not?

Question: How is your church evangelized as well as evangelizing?

Question: In what way is your church one in which people will see the body of Christ? What prevents them seeing him?

KINGDOM

6. Evangelization — building the kingdom

If we look at the life of Jesus we notice that his primary proclamation concerns the coming of the Kingdom of God. Jesus uses many stories to describe what it means to belong to that Kingdom and the way in which it is built up. He also highlights the demands that inheriting the Kingdom brings with it. Now, Christians are into the Kingdom-building business in a big way — or at least we should be. So, what can we say about this Kingdom and what are our responsibilities in the task of enabling it to come about 'on earth as it is in heaven'? Clearly the Kingdom has nothing to do with states or geographical boundaries. It has something to do with the reign of God in the lives of individuals and something to do with society.

We should note four things about the Kingdom. The first is that we can describe it as the reign of God. That reign consists of justice, faithfulness and freedom. The second is that his reign is not confined to the spiritual dimension but is to 'come on earth as it is in heaven'. It is to be created in the reality of the physical world in which we live. Clearly in a world in which millions are starving, condemned to poverty or unjustly imprisoned the Kingdom has not come. Thirdly, the Kingdom is both present and yet to come. There are times and places where justice does prevail and where liberty is attained. In these areas the reign of God is present; it is here in our world but only in part. As injustice and captivity still exist it has not come in all its fullness. So, we can say that the Kingdom is already moving among us in the here and now but it has still to come in all its fullness. Fourthly, the task of enabling the Kingdom to come rests with us. Our task is to be channels through which the Kingdom can more fully come — through our actions and words and life. Anything we do to free people from any sort of oppression, physical or mental; anything that enhances the dignity of another human being or anything that rights a wrong, enables the Kingdom to come. Wherever the Church (and ourselves as individual members of it) works for justice and integrity, where she stands up for the rights of the poor and the marginalized, where she proclaims the Gospel values of integrity and respect for creation, there the Kingdom is coming. It is not present in all its richness but it is present. We are journeying towards it and have a responsibility for enabling it to come about. We have already seen that evangelization has to do with challenging society as well as proclaiming the Gospel to individuals. So, evangelization cannot be divorced from building the Kingdom nor can working for social justice be divorced from evangelization.

This awareness that the Church is called to co-operate with God in establishing his reign on earth is not only a global issue. It applies to the local Christian community and to individuals within it. In our own situations we have a responsibility to find ways of allowing the Kingdom to come into the reality of our area. In the next section we shall look more closely at our own communities and the way in which we are called to journey on the path of faith and share that journey with others. We need to ask ourselves how we are involved in the Kingdom-building work which God is doing. Here is an exercise to get us going.

Group work on the theme: Building the kingdom

Step 1
Ask for the guidance of God on your meeting.

Step 2
Read Matthew 13:31–32.

Step 3
Spend a few moments in silence thinking of your church as a mustard tree.

Step 4
Go through the parable using the questions below and develop a picture of your church in the light of it. You may wish to do this by drawing a tree and putting in the roots, the trunk, the branches and the surrounding area.

The kingdom of Heaven is like a mustard seed which a man took and sowed in his field.

Looking at your church community, how has the seed of the Kingdom, the reign of God, been sown?

(a) in your church?
(b) through your church?

It is the smallest of all the seeds.

What roots have you put down which are nourishing you as a community?

But when it is grown it is the biggest of shrubs and becomes a tree.

Where has the Kingdom grown in your church?

So that the birds of the air can come and shelter in its branches.

Who do you shelter?
Who might you shelter that you do not at present?

Step 5
What are you going to do about what you have learned?

Step 6
Ask God to lead you.

Our church on the move

One big area which every local Christian community needs to consider is whether or not our church is really on the move or whether it is simply static. We also need to ask ourselves how well our church relates to the community around us and how we are involved in building up the Kingdom within it. Do we spend all our time and energy with our internal agenda or are we conscious of the context in which our local community exists, allowing it to affect the way we think and act in our evangelistic task? In other words, what sort of mentality do we have? Is it static or is it outward-looking? Is it a mentality that welcomes pilgrimage and sees in movement opportunities for growth, or is it a fortress mentality, pulling up the drawbridges, shutting ourselves away and hoping that the world will not impinge upon us too much?

> Evangelization implies enthusiasm and apostolic zeal in the procla-
> mation of the Gospel, a passionate desire to help people fall in love
> with Jesus and commit themselves to him forever. More than a
> programme, evangelization is an attitude. It is a mentality of sharing,
> of inviting, of welcoming people into the joy of communion with
> Jesus Christ.
>
> (Texas Bishops, *Pastoral Letter on Evangelization*)

Unless we can be honest with ourselves and face the questions about our attitude and mentality we shall be hampered in the task of proclaiming the Gospel to those around us. But facing these questions is often difficult and threatening. That is why people like to latch on to a programme. It is much easier to contain evangelization in a programme than to face the fact that it should be a lifestyle and a mentality. Such an attitude demands openness and flexibility and a willingness to change.

Question: In my local church how much time is spent on internal issues and how much in concern for the wider community?

Question: How much 'desire to help people fall in love with Jesus' can be seen in your church?

One of the difficulties that many churches face is discerning how to move in order to remain both faithful to the past and yet faithful to the call of God to the future. When St Anne's decided to alter their Sunday Mass to include more songs which would be enjoyed by the young people who met in the hall afterwards, all did not go well. There were many who said the worship was being 'trivialized' and others who threatened to leave because 'these young people only come for the music'. It is all too simple to make the wrong decision one way or the other. It is easy to remain as we have always been and to try to shut out the world around us, refusing to change or to be influenced by those whose world we share. On the other hand it is easy, especially if we feel guilty that we are not doing anything, to rush into activities which are neither relevant nor particularly helpful to those around us. In our anxiety to be seen to have a message for today, we can easily fly headlong into activities which may well be neither the most useful nor the most constructive. Such activities often drain us of energy and, because we have not looked carefully at the world around us, may be doomed to failure before they start. Such failures just drive us more and more deeply into an attitude of mind in which we refuse to make ourselves vulnerable again and where our local churches cease to move forward. The result is an inward-looking and static community.

It is sometimes difficult to develop an outward-looking mentality and it can be a frightening and threatening process to open ourselves up to the world around us in order to proclaim the Gospel. It is much easier to keep ourselves to ourselves, safe in our own security. Yet, if we look at the life of Jesus we see that this is not what he did. His whole attitude was one of outward movement.

Question: How do you see this movement out to others expressed in the life of Jesus?

Jesus proclaimed that the Kingdom had come in the midst of the ordinary, everyday life of the world around him. It was there among all the tensions and anxieties of daily living that the Gospel was preached. All local churches are called to follow this example and unless we are willing to do so and to meet the world where it is, rather than travel along parallel lines, we are unfaithful to the Christ who sends us into his world.

Group work on the theme:
Our church on the move

Step 1
Pray together.

Step 2
On your own list what you like about your church. List what you dislike.

(Compare your lists with the other people in the group. Are there likes and dislikes in common?)

Step 3
Sometimes our likes and dislikes happen as a result of change. We may dislike a change or we may like it. Discuss:

- How many of your likes and dislikes are the result of change in your church?
- How would you go about the process of change?
- Who would be involved, how would you do it?
- How would you prepare people for this change?
- How would you cope with conflict and opposite views?

Step 5
Look back over the way your church has changed in the last ten years.

In prayer: thank God for the changes for the better; ask for his forgiveness for any hurt caused or wrong decisions.

Journeying to the future

No journey takes place without some idea of the goal to which we are progressing. The journey in faith, both as individuals and as communities, is undertaken because we believe that God wishes us and others to have fullness of life. We hope and pray that we are moving towards a situation in which the Kingdom has come more fully and the life of Christ is more readily recognized among us. In other words we have an aim, a goal, a vision of the future.

It is important to dream, to have visions, to hold before us a picture of what we long to be. The prophet Joel recognized this clearly, 'Your sons and daughters shall prophesy, your old people dream dreams, and your young people see visions' (Joel 3:1). Having a dream or a vision is not an idle waste of time, provided the dream is based on the Gospel and not totally removed from an awareness of the reality in which we live. As individuals and as groups we can dream dreams. As individual members of the body of Christ what do we long to be? What do we long to do? As members of the community that makes up the universal Church what dreams do we have for our local church? What do we hope it might do in our situation? How do we want it to be? As we ask ourselves these questions there are two things that we should remember about this vision or dream for the future.

A vision of the gospel

The first is that these dreams must have the quality of the visionary about them. They should not be daydreams. Daydreams are an escape from reality. In developing our local community we must not fall into this trap. To dream of the future is not to escape into some sort of world that can never be. We should not try to 'dream the impossible dream'. Such a vision is bound to lead to disappointment in the end. Nor can we have a dream in order to opt out of being involved in the nitty-gritty of the world in which we live. We dare not use the excuse of having a vision of the future to escape the difficulties of the present. Nor must we use the excuse of dreaming a dream in order to shift the blame for our present failures or mistakes on to someone or something else. Rather, we are called to have a dream which is based on the Gospel; a Gospel which is about the Incarnation, about being involved in this world. Our dream must be about a life and a community lived in all its fullness in the reality of the present situation, not an escape from it.

A vision for all

The second thing we must note about this vision for the future is that it must never be exclusive. The dreams we have for ourselves and for our church must have within them an openness and a willingness to think in broad terms. No dream based on the Gospel can be exclusive. Unfortunately, many of our communities fall down on this point. The vision we have, if we have one at all, is too narrow and concerned only with our own identity and survival. But this is not what the proclamation of the Kingdom is all about. We do not have to look far for a warning against this exclusive attitude. In the Old Testament the prophet Jonah presents us with a strong message that God is not to be bound into little boxes and cannot be confined within an exclusive framework. The call is to preach to the wider world, represented by the Ninevites. Jonah objects to this request from God and tries to run away. Somewhat reluctantly he at last does so. But his annoyance that God should care for these people who were beyond the pale and be willing to forgive them, bubbles over at the end of the book where we see Jonah going off in a sulk: who should receive God's love and God's compassion is beyond his limited understanding.

Jonah's concept of God was narrow, confined. His vision was only of his own community. We dare not let this happen to us. Similarly, if we look at the life of Jesus we see that he was not into confining the love of God. His vision of the Kingdom was one in which the smallest of all the seeds becomes the greatest of trees and 'all the birds of the air can come and rest under its branches'. His very dealings with women and men should be enough to keep us continually on our guard against too narrow a vision of what it means for our community to proclaim the Gospel.

Question: How narrow is your vision of the church?

What would happen if the equivalent of the Ninevites came to your church?

If the Gospel is for all what does this mean, in practice, for the way your local church evangelizes?

Group work on the theme:
Journeying to the future

Step 1
Split the group into threes. Give each group a large sheet of paper and ask them to draw their church community. This should be a representation of the community as it is *now* — not how they imagine it to be or long for it to be.

Step 2
Give people the chance to look at one another's drawings.

Step 3
Discuss together what the pictures say about your local church.

Step 4
One person reads 1 Corinthians 12:4–31.

Step 5
In the light of the passage and what has been said about a vision for your local church, ask the same small groups to draw how they would like their church to be. Encourage them to dream dreams and see visions.

Step 6
Display the pictures and discuss together what is being said about the sort of Christian community which they envisage for the future.

Step 7
Pick three common themes that have come from the pictures and discuss how these might begin to be put into practice. Make sure that any plans you make in the light of your vision are attainable.

Step 8
Close with a prayer for the guidance of the Holy Spirit on the work you hope to undertake.

(Adapted from Christine Dodd, *Making Scripture Work*, p. 43.)

Chapter 4

CALLED FOR THE WORLD
Listening and working with God in his world

1. Our church, our world

So far we have concentrated on what we might call the 'internal' side of the Church's life. We have thought about the journey of the pilgrim people of God and the task we have of travelling with others along their path. We must now look more closely at the relationship between our local church and the world outside its doors.

The first thing we must recognize is our in-built tendency to make a dividing line between Church and world. In some cases this can become almost a 'them and us' mentality. Sometimes we do this because the world then seems less threatening, less challenging and it gives us a much safer feeling to keep the two apart. If we can mentally keep 'them' on the other side of our dividing line then we can remain in our comfortable little world. Such a mentality also gives us the excuse of placing the blame for lack of involvement of 'them' squarely on 'their' shoulders. If they wish to come and cross our dividing line we will welcome them with open arms but they must make the move; they must cross over into our world. For huge numbers of people such a leap is not only unlikely, it is almost impossible. It is impossible because they have never experienced church and often they see no reason why they should! Even if people are attracted to our community the courage that is required to step into a strange body of people and become involved is extremely difficult to find. Very few people actually do this unless they know someone who is already within that community or unless part of that community has gone out to them. Before we progress any further it is a good idea to try to see the importance of this.

Exercise
To attempt to understand just what it might be like to be a stranger coming into your community try to imagine yourself as someone

with no particular Christian understanding walking into your church for the first time. Try to see it through his or her eyes.

(a) What sort of initial impact do you receive from the building itself? Is it dark or light, welcoming or discouraging?
(b) What sort of welcome do you receive from the people? Does it really exist? Is it warm? Is it overpowering?
(c) What is expected of you? Are you given masses of books or papers you are expected to read and find your way around?
(d) Where are you to sit? Do you have to walk all the way to the front in the full gaze of everyone to get a seat? Are you left to fend for yourself?
(e) Does what goes on have any real relevance to your life and to your lived experience?
(f) What happens afterwards?

Remember: Try to do this as an outsider, coming to your community for the first time. When you have done the exercise perhaps you may wish to talk over what improvements you might be able to make.

It is important now that we consider the relationship between Church and world and begin to see it in more positive terms. Rather than seeing it as a chasm, which people have to jump over in order to join us, we should see it as an *interface* or meeting point between us. This is the point at which our two communities meet. It is a point at which there are enormous opportunities for us to proclaim the Gospel. But they will only be opportunities for us if we cease to have a 'them and us' mentality. They will only be opportunities if we begin to see that what exists is not a dividing line but a bridge.

It is important that we get our thinking clear about this meeting point because, unless we do, our evangelization will suffer. If we see the Church only as a place to which we can run in order to escape from involvement in the world or feel that society at large is to be avoided, that is bound to have a knock-on effect on our evangelization.

Group work on the theme: Our church, our world

Step 1
Have a short time of prayer together asking for God's guidance.

Step 2
A group member should read the following:

John became involved some time ago in the town photographic society which met on Wednesday evenings. When he decided to spend the next Wednesday at the society's meeting, the local prayer group were not pleased. John had promised to take Kevin, his great friend, to the meeting site because demolition contractors were coming in to blow up an old building and they both wanted the chance to photograph the event. Wednesday was the day the prayer group always met so his absence would be noted, but John carefully explained that Kevin could not drive and it was not safe for him to be in that area of town alone. Some people secretly accused John of not taking his commitment to the prayer group seriously, and others said this hobby had nothing to do with John's Christianity. They thought he should get his priorities sorted out: after all, prayer was more important than taking photographs.

Step 3
Discuss the story in the light of your own experiences of church and secular activities.

   (a) What do you see as the tensions in the story?
   (b) Do you or the people in your church suffer similar tensions?
   (c) What do you think is your attitude to the world/church connection?

Step 4
Reflect on your attitude to the relationship between your faith lived out in the local church and your faith lived out in the rest of your life.

Step 5
Read Romans 8:35–39 as a closing prayer.

2. Listening to the world

There are two vital tasks which the local church community must undertake if its relationship with the world at large is to be a realistic one. First, it must listen to the world and find out what God is saying within it. Second, it must enter into dialogue with the wider world in order to proclaim the Gospel.

Just as it is wrong to think of a huge chasm between the

church and the world over which people must jump if they are to become members of our community, so it is also wrong to believe or to act as if God can only be discovered within the Church. God's activity extends far beyond the Church's boundaries. Therefore, it is important that we try to see him beyond those boundaries. If we can see where he is at work in his world then we can begin to *co-operate* with him. This concept of co-operation with God in the world is vital. As we have seen in Chapter 1, it means that our evangelization should be spoken of less in terms of taking Christ to others so much as helping others to discover the Christ who is already there. A great deal of evangelization is about helping people to open their eyes to the God who is already at work within them. And God *is* at work there if only we had eyes to see him.

Mary suffered badly from depression. When asked what helped her to cope she replied that it was a combination of her family's support and the techniques she had discovered for dealing with what she called her 'dark clouds'. When it was bad she would wake up in the morning feeling totally unable to face the day and wishing only for the oblivion of sleep or death. Then she would make a bargain with herself to cope with the first two hours, and when those two hours were up to do the same for the next two. 'I get through it somehow', she said. 'I look back and I am amazed that I did it; that I had the strength and courage to cope. Where it comes from I have no idea I only know it works.' I have no doubt that God is at work in Mary's situation. Helping her to see that is part of the process of evangelization. It is helping her to see the Christ who is with her in all the horror of her depression, and it is helping her to give him a name.

It is not only seeing how God is at work in the lives of individuals that should concern us. We should also be concerned about how God is at work in society as a whole. Evangelization is about Kingdom-building. When Jesus talks about the Kingdom of God he is not really talking about a geographical space but about the coming of God's goodness in all its fullness. He is talking about the reign of God. Evangelization is about seeing the signs of the Kingdom; those areas where God's rule is coming within the society in which we live. It is about co-operating with God in his work within that society in order that the Kingdom may be more fully present. This means that the members of the local church must be willing to get involved in organizations and societies which are not specifically religious.

Let us go back to Mary and her depression. The self-help group she belongs to is not religious and is not affiliated in any way to the Church, yet the fact that this is where new freedom, support and hope can be found is a sure sign that here God is at work. Paul *is* a member of a church and he too suffers from depression. He is involved in the group and by being so his presence is a help both to him and to other members of the group to which he belongs. His awareness that God is with him in his depression enables him to make that known to others in a similar situation.

By involving ourselves in this way we are not only able to see where God is already at work, we are able to allow him to use us as instruments in order for that work to be continued and to grow. In other words, we allow him to evangelize through us.

This openness to seeing God at work in the wider world can have two important effects on our Christian community. First, it can give a much needed boost. Seeing the many and varied ways in which God is at work helps stop us from slipping into any form of pessimism. If we open our eyes and ears we shall see his work all around us in so many ways that it will astound us. Second, our willingness to see this and to respond to the activity of God in the lives of individuals and in society will send a very clear message to those who come into contact with us. It states that this group of people is not 'so heavenly minded they are no earthly use'. Rather, it will be said that here is a group of people who take real life very seriously and who see that God is involved in that life and immersed within it. It will be clearly saying that God is concerned with real people in real situations; that he can be found there, and that his life can be part of our own.

How do we know that God is in the world?

One final but vital point needs to be made regarding this discovery of God in the world he has created. It is of the essence of the Good News that Christ came and lived among us. By doing this God has stated in an action that has far more impact than words ever can, how much he is involved in the world he has made; how much he loves it and us, and the lengths to which he is willing to go in order that we might discover the treasures that he has in store for us. It is the whole life of Christ that proclaims so strongly God's involvement with his creation.

If we are to proclaim the true Gospel then we must take seriously that the Good News we have concerns this very involvement. If we truly believe in the message of the Incarnation, 'God with us', then discovering the signs of God outside our church boundaries, seeing him all around us and being involved in that world is a necessity not an optional extra. To withdraw from it or to refuse to see God within it is to be untrue to the Gospel we have been given.

Evangelization is about concern for and active involvement with God in his world. We need to 'do' the Gospel as well as to 'talk' the Gospel, but to 'do' we must first listen to what God is saying to us through the needs of our world. There is no excuse for not listening and no corner of the world that is not our concern.

Group work on the theme: Listening to the world

Step 1
Begin with a prayer.

Step 2
Read the following story.

> Margarida is a Brazilian widow. She has five children. Every morning she gets up at three o'clock and walks six miles to work. There, she spends four hours heaving rocks to build a dam. Her monthly pay is £8. 'When I leave home, I have a bit of coffee with manioc flour, that's all. Hunger pains begin about 10 o'clock but you have to put up with them. The ones who can't just collapse. I have seen lots of women collapse on to the rocks. We earn next to nothing, but my work is the only thing between us and death.'

Margarida is not alone. Millions like her live at the bottom of the pile, trapped by the massive injustice of the world. You are probably near to the top of the pile. Most people reading this book will be well clothed, fed, watered and housed.

Meanwhile . . .

- Ten children a minute die of diarrhoea.
- Six out of seven people do not have clean running water.
- 35,000 people a day die because they haven't enough food.
- Every fortnight the world spends £12 billion on arms.

Step 3

God speaks to us through these facts. What is your reaction to this? How does it make you feel? Discuss.

Step 4

Listen to God's word

> Is not this the kind of fasting I have chosen: to loose the chains of injustice and untie the cords of the yoke, to set the oppressed free and break every yoke? . . . If you spend yourselves on behalf of the hungry and satisfy the needs of the oppressed then your light will rise in the darkness, and your night will become like the noonday.
>
> (Isaiah 58:6, 10)

Step 5

Look at this 'involvement' scale. On your own put a tick where you think you are now and another where you would like to be in six months' time.

☐ Unaware of world issues.
☐ Beginning to find out more.
☐ Actively wanting to find out more.
☐ Beginning to realize that I can do something.
☐ Knowing I can do something but wondering what.
☐ Writing to my MP.
☐ Supporting an aid agency with my money.
☐ Supporting an aid agency with my time.
☐ Other action . . .

● Share with each other 'where you are at'.
● Share with each other where you would like to be.
● What should you do to move forward? What should your church do?

Step 6

End with a time of prayer committing all that you have learned to God.

(Adapted from Tim Mayfield, *Thank God for That!*, Bible Reading Fellowship.)

3. Conversing with God in his world

So far we have seen how important it is to discover how God acts both within and outside our church boundaries. But watching him at work and seeing how he acts is not enough. If we are truly to co-operate with his activity, and therefore to allow him to use us as instruments within his work of evangelization, then we must be willing to take the step of entering into dialogue with him in the world that he has made. It is not enough to be concerned about Margarida, we have to put our concern into action.

Listening to God in the world

This entering into dialogue should have two effects on us. The first is that dialogue requires an openness and a willingness to listen and consequently to be *changed* by what we have heard. There can be no conversation if the movement is all one way. Of its nature a dialogue involves give and take; listening and speaking. Therefore, the first effect that communicating with the wider world should have on us is that we should learn from it as well as having something to put into the process ourselves. It is through interacting with people who may not be connected with our church or with people of other Christian traditions or other faiths or with our involvement in various non-church organizations that we ourselves shall be evangelized as well as being evangelizers. If God is truly at work in these situations then our contact with him should enable us to learn more about him and to respond to him in new ways. In its turn this willingness to allow God to evangelize us through his activity elsewhere will save us from the false belief that we can have God all neatly packaged-up and that we know where he is and is not at work. We shall cease to be surprised when he continually breaks out of the boxes into which we put him or when we discover his activity in areas we had not imagined. It will also save us from that dreadful sin of pride in thinking that we have some sort of hotline or private information about where God is and is not at work and about where it is possible to enter into conversation with him. This awareness of his overarching activity can be both releasing and threatening. Discovering him at work in the photographic club or the local day centre can open new vistas for us but it can also frighten us for we must expect then to see him everywhere. There is no escape from his presence. We will find him not only in our churches but in our leisure activities, at a football match or at the cinema. We will find him wherever there are people, even if the outward signs make it seem unlikely. We will find him in our prisons, in our hostels for the homeless, in our hospitals and in our schools, theatres, casinos, mountainsides, House of Commons . . .

Question: Do I see God in unlikely places? Where?

Question: How do I recognize him?

Question: How do I respond to him there?

The second effect this entering into communication with individuals and society can have is on the *way* in which we begin to evangelize. Once we begin to see God at work in the world and we begin to co-operate with him and to enter into dialogue with the society in which we live then our evangelization takes on a very different shape and form. It becomes not so much a 'taking Christ to people' as a discovery of where he is already at work and helping people to open their eyes to him. It is pointing out the Christ who is already there.

Giving a name to the God who is there

This proclamation of the Gospel involves a lot of 'naming'. Here we are in the process of enabling people to name the Good News that is already there and to discover and name that which they had not recognized as Good News. For instance, evangelization took place when Mary was helped to put a name to the strength she felt was with her in times of depression.

This task is just as demanding as a form of evangelization which is more 'up front'. Indeed in some ways it is much more demanding. The very direct and obviously explicit form of evangelization has the great advantage of being relatively neat and tidy. It does not necessarily demand entering into dialogue with those around us in any depth. Unfortunately, it can also mean that people fail to see the relevance of the Good News; that we scratch where people do not itch and that we give them solutions to questions they are not asking. A form of evangelization which involves helping people see the Christ who is already there, is much less neat and tidy. It demands that we listen seriously to those with whom we are in contact.

It can challenge us because their questions can challenge us and can involve us in a long and sometimes quite slow process which enables them to discover the reality and relevance of a God who is already at work within them. Proclaiming the Gospel without taking into account the situation and the context of the hearers may, in some ways, seem more appealing and more forthright but it is not necessarily the best way for our local communities to proceed.

Group work on the theme: Conversing with God in his world

Here is an exercise designed to help us 'name' the God within us and see how the process of evangelization is lifelong.

Step 1
Invite the group to spend a few moments in silence. Ask for the help of the Holy Spirit.

Step 2
Think of your life as a road-map and see if you can draw it. It should contain:

— Important turnings and decisions in your life.
— Important people in your life who have directed you in certain directions.
— The areas in your life where you think you have gone backwards.
— Times when you think you have been 'all at sea'.
— Times when you have been closely aware of God's presence with you.
— 'Outside' non-religious influences in which you now see that God was at work leading you.
— Times when you have been a map for other people.

Mountains and valleys could be included in your map. Use your imagination over this exercise.

Step 3
Can you see how God has worked in *different ways*, at *different speeds* and through *different people*?

Can you see the intimate relation between God, his creation, and you?

Step 4
Share as much or as little of your map as you wish with others.
What does this 'conversing with God in his world' say about how
we evangelize and are evangelized?

Step 5
Read the story of Abraham on his journey (Genesis 12:1–5) as a
closing prayer.

4. At work in the world

We must now turn to the question of how all we have said about
dialogue with the wider community and individuals within it
can be translated into action by the local church. The first thing
we need to note here is that most of our evangelization will not
in fact be happening within the church context. It will be
through individual Christians in dialogue with others, proclaiming the Gospel wherever they are. That may be at work or
through involvement in various organizations, clubs and societies, or through their leisure activities. Unfortunately, as a local
church, we very often fail to see involvement in these activities
as part of our Christian life together. We tend to think that
our church organizations are the only ones through which the
Gospel can be proclaimed.

It is no bad thing therefore to look occasionally at what people
are actually *doing* outside their church involvement and to recognize just how much activity does go on. Furthermore, we
should be *encouraging* people to be involved in such a way.
Again it is unfortunate that we so often put all our energies
into encouraging people to join various church groups and
organizations and hardly any into encouraging them to join
secular groups in which they could be a Christian influence.
We should stress the need for people to have the right balance
in their lives in the way they spend their time. They need time
on their own, they need time for leisure activity, they need time
to be with other Christians and, of course, they need time with
their families. It is when this balance gets upset (and it can
easily be upset by undue pressure being exerted by the local
church community) that things can go dangerously wrong. We
should be encouraging people seriously to consider their use of
time and to make informed decisions as to where they should
spend it. We should not be in the business of making some

people feel guilty if they choose to spend some of their time within a secular organization because they feel that that is where God is leading them and that is where they can be of influence, rather than spending their time within our church group.

Question: How do you use your time — is the balance right?

Question: Is your church encouraging people to be involved in secular activities?

Question: Does your church make undue demands on people, or not enough demands, or about right?

It is not just individuals who should be in dialogue with the wider world but whole church communities. In many ways our local churches are ideally placed as 'meeting points' between the world God has made and its creator. Sometimes we are supremely placed simply because of the buildings and physical facilities we have at our disposal. If we use our resources only for 'churchy' activities then we could be missing out on a glorious opportunity of proclaiming the Gospel to others. Very many local churches have found this advantage in allowing their buildings to be used by all sorts of secular groups, thereby coming into contact with them and with the people that make up those groups. So our local churches can offer very tangible and physical help to those in the society in which we live.

The local group of the Samaritans, the organization which exists to offer counselling and help to the depressed and those who feel tempted to suicide, was looking for premises. St Mark's had the ideal solution. They had room. They had a central location, they even had people who would be willing to become involved within the work of the Samaritans. At first, there was some reluctance to allow a group that was not affiliated in any way to the church to use the premises. This was gradually overcome. The same sort of reluctance was felt down the road at St Joseph's where a request was received from the local Natural History club for the use of part of their crypt which had recently been redecorated and re-ordered to provide meeting places. Openness to the possibility of using our buildings in an imaginative and constructive way for the use of the wider community has much to say about our attitude towards them and also has something to say about how wide we see the task of evangelization.

Responding to the community

The local church can also be a meeting point in another way. It can actively reach out as a community to others and initiate all sorts of activities which will involve it in dialogue with others. To do this of course it must be aware of the needs within the community it seeks to serve (and not what it *thinks* the needs are). However, once the needs have been discerned then it is possible to initiate and begin activities in order to help meet those needs and in order to enter into conversation with others. So, a local church may have discovered that within its area there are huge numbers of young families and particularly young parents with very little provision made for them to come together with facilities for children to play. The parents within that community decide that this is a real need and that something could be done about it by the local church. So, they begin a Toddler Group which brings within the church orbit a whole range of young parents and children who might not otherwise darken its doors. Through the involvement of local church members within this group, individuals come to express their own questioning and their own difficulties, joys and sorrows, and a dialogue is established which enables many people to see where God is already at work within them and where he might also be discovered in new ways.

Group work on the theme:
At work in the world

We have stressed in this chapter the importance of listening and acting in real dialogue and concern for the world around us. We have also stressed that it is important to discern what those needs are if our evangelization is to be effective. There are many ways of doing this. Here is one suggestion. It will take you several meetings to do it and will involve work between meetings but, if it is done properly, it will open a whole new vista for the evangelistic task of the local church community.

YOUR AREA

Step 1
Map your area. Things to have on the basic map:

ROADS

The primary element is the road network shown at three levels (so far as they apply).

(a) Major roads such as commuter and transportation routes (red).
(b) Important town or neighbourhood roads (yellow).
(c) Other streets: mainly residential, access roads (uncoloured).
(d) Add bus stops (lollipop symbol).
(e) Add railway lines (black) and stations if any.

BUILDINGS

Mark churches, parks, public buildings, shops, schools etc.

HOUSING

Mark housing by colour — private, council, private rented, high rise.

RESIDENTS

Write in:

OP — elderly residents
YM — young marrieds
MA — middle-aged
S   — single.

ETHNIC GROUPS

Write across relevant areas. Where there is no clear predominance, indicate what the trend is in each part of your area.

DEMOLITION AREAS

Waste land, old sites, demolished buildings or condemned buildings or blocks should be indicated by black dots, with a label.

ANY OTHER FEATURES

Indicate and label — use your imagination about what you should include.

YOUR COMMUNITY

Step 2
Supplement the map with a brief comment about the following:

PEOPLE

1. Who are they? Elderly, middle-aged, young married, single?
2. What sort of jobs do they have? Where do they work?
3. Why are they there? Degree of choice/coercion.
4. How long have they been there? Stability/mobility.
5. What do they look for outside the area?

6. Where do they come from? Places of birth and upbringing.

RELATIONSHIPS

1. What do people do together? e.g. institutions, clubs, associations, dominant local politics, informal groups.
2. Who is respected, feared, considered significant — and why?
3. How do people get along with each other? Within groups? Between groups?

PERCEPTIONS

1. How is the place seen by the residents?
2. How is the place seen by people from outside the area? By the professionals (planners, estate agents, social workers, police, teachers, clergy)? By you?
3. How do the residents see other places, and outsiders?
4. What myths about the area are there?
5. What do people complain about?
6. What are people proud of, or pleased about?

RECENT EXPERIENCES

1. When recently have people acted together to achieve something?
2. Which people have acted? For change, or to preserve the status quo?
3. Is anyone trying to identify the needs and potential of the community?
4. Who is determining the shape of your community? Who are the people making the decisions?
5. What groups or people or parties or departments impose their will on the community?
6. What changes have you seen in your area? Who made them? Who opposed them? Who won? Whose side were you on?
7. What attitude did/does your church take to these movements or developments?

LIFESTYLE

1. Are there conflicts of lifestyle in the community? Specify.
2. What assumptions and values are indicated by the way groups of people live?
3. Are there 'top' people and 'bottom' people? When it came to the crunch, whose side were you on?

You could discover the answers to these questions by:

INFORMAL METHODS

1. Hanging around pubs, talking outside schools, in shops, launderettes, welfare centres, clinics, etc.
2. Identifying people in the centre of a communication-web.
3. Finding those to whom people turn for help.
4. Getting into the culture of the community.

FORMAL METHODS

1. Surveys, questionnaires, statistics, census data, household surveys.
2. Interviews, conversations, group work.
3. Photographs, films, tape recordings, histories, newspapers.

YOUR CHURCH

Step 3

THE SITUATION

1. What churches are involved in the area?
2. What ecclesiastical structures and boundaries are there in the area?
3. List the people belonging to each local church:
   (a) *Staff ordained and lay*
       i names
       ii responsibilities
       iii place of residence
       iv age, families etc.
   (b) *Lay leadership*
       i 10–12 key laymen/laywomen
       ii their age, residence, secular jobs, church jobs.
   (c) *Church members*
       By numbers, sex and age: 12–19, 20–29, 30–44, 45–49, 50–59, 60–70+; indicate major residence areas on map.
   (d) *Fringe members or irregular attenders*
       List as above.

THE ACTIVITIES

1. *Worship*
   Average number morning and evening, age, and sex. What percentage worship both mornings and evenings? Number of normal communicants.

2. *Activities*
   Sunday school, uniformed organizations and other groups: frequency, numbers attending, location of homes.

3. *Premises*
   Date of buildings, accommodation description, capacity, present condition and purposes used for.

4. *Finance*
   i present financial position
   ii past two years' accounts
   iii next year's budget
   iv forward forecast.

THE CHURCH MEMBERS

1. Economic status and social position.
2. Place of origin and mobility.
3. Cultural interests.
4. Length of association.
5. Place of residence.
6. Age, sex etc. relative to area.

PORTRAIT OF THE CHURCH COMMUNITY

1. Relationship of leadership to congregation.
2. Number and nature of worshippers involved in other church activities.
3. Level of participation — who, how and when of participation.
4. Recent history of the church — buildings, amalgamations, events, campaigns.
5. Cliques or affinity groups.
6. Decision-making, theoretically and practically.
7. Involvement of church in wider community
   (a) individuals
   (b) groups
   (c) whole church.
8. Involvement of wider community in church events.
9. Ecumenical involvement and its significance.
10. What is going on that you would not expect?
11. Religious ethos: What is the overall feeling? What is the impact on a stranger?
12. Extent to which the officiant determines quality of service and feel of liturgy.
13. To what extent do the people practise the same religion as the officiant?
14. What is the 'folk religion' in the congregation or sections of it?
15. What is the role of the church school (if present)?

THE CHURCH AND THE WORLD

1. What else is going on in the area of Christian significance, e.g. non-church groups, para-church groups, community-concern groups, care-of-needy groups, political issue groups, school/parent associations?
2. What else is going on in the community which impinges on the church or Christian scene?
3. How does the church's work impinge on the world, the place and the community as you have analysed them?
4. Who holds power in the world, place and community as you analysed them? Do you have powerful or powerless people? Or both? Who, specifically?
5. What, in your world, place and community is the church supporting? (Good or bad?) What is it trying to change? What could it support? Or change?

WHEN YOU'VE DONE IT ALL

Step 4
At the end when you've got it all assembled and written up, get the group together again and ask them to write lists of the good things and the bad things — and then vote on them to get an order of priority and a 'Top ten'. Then list them:

1. Ten things for sorrow in our community/church/world.

2. Ten things for joy in our community/church/world.

Then perhaps you'll begin to say, 'We could do something about . . . couldn't we?'

Step 5
Make plans for the future.

Reprinted, with alterations, by permission from Dr John Vincent, *Situation Analysis* (Sheffield: Urban Theology Unit).

Chapter 5

CALLED TO PROCLAIM
Discovering our gifts

We noted in Chapter 1 the principle that the Church, by her nature, is evangelizing and being evangelized. She exists in order to evangelize. We also saw that the task is one for every member of the Body of Christ. *Every* Christian, not just clergy, religious or the 'professional' lay person has his or her unique part to play.

> Evangelization is, to a large degree, simply sharing the riches of the faith we have . . . Our Lord Jesus Christ depends on all the baptized to carry on this work of evangelization.
>
> (Texas Bishops, *Pastoral Letter on Evangelization*)

The ways in which this evangelization is carried out within the local church community will be many and varied. However, there are two areas which are worth exploring in order to clear the ground. The first concerns the teaching of the Church on the role of the laity and its implication for evangelization. The second concerns the working out of that role in practice within the local church.

1. The laity and evangelization

Lay people in the Church

For lay people there is a two-fold task to fulfil. First, there is the role of the lay person within the life of the worshipping community itself. Second, the lay person has a role in the wider world. The Christian community should be one which, by its very nature and life, is an evangelizing one. When people come to us or see us 'in action' they should be attracted to what they see. If the community is basing its life on Gospel values then it should raise questions for people about what the community is doing. Why does it exist? Why is the community the way it is? How come these people seem to have something extra? For that to happen the community must truly be just that — a real community in which everyone is treated with equal dignity, is respected and plays a full part. Unfortunately, very many of our local church communities are not like this at all. They are anything but attractive to outsiders. They are filled with factions and disagreements and often with passive members. Sometimes that is the fault of the leadership within the community but often it is the fault of the members themselves.

St Michael's has a large church congregation and a great deal goes on through its activities. The problem St Michael's has arises partly from history, partly from its members and partly from the leadership. The result is that within St Michael's there is one group that tends to do everything and run everything. This group are the 'old-stagers' in terms of the length of time they have been in the congregation and they are reluctant to let others share the leadership with them. The difficulty is not made any better by the fact that the minister in the church tends to rely on this group because he knows them and because he does not want to cause the conflict which would undoubtedly arise if he encouraged new people to become involved. Many of the rest of the church feel left out, unwanted and useless. This sort of divided community inevitably fails to be the welcoming group which enables people to come within it, discover their gifts and use their talents through it.

Strength for the task

Added to this need for our local Christian communities to be attractive to others, we need to note that the church also should be a place where people receive strength and a new heart for the task they have within the wider world. Evangelization is to be carried out within the ordinary everyday situations of our lives. Whether it is at work, at home, or in our leisure activities, the task of living up to Gospel values and answering questions where they are asked is the task that we all hold in common. Such a responsibility and a privilege is not easy, and we need the strength and the comradeship which being with our fellow Christians gives us.

The local Christian community therefore has a dual function: to be evangelized herself within her own life, and to give strength to her members in their own responsibilities within the wider world. So St Michael's needs not only to be a welcoming community where all are accepted, but a place where those members of God's family who worship there may receive new strength for their witness in their everyday lives.

Question: How 'open' is your church? Is it divided in any way?

Question: Do people find a ready welcome?

Question: Do they find it attractive?

Question: What strength do you gain from being with one another?

Lay people in the wider world

It is within this wider world that the second great task of lay people exists. Because we, the laity, spend most of our time in the wider world, making Christ real there is our responsibility.

> Evangelists are very ordinary people witnessing among ordinary persons who live and work around them, sharing with them their own story of coming to a new experience of joy and freedom. Neighbours seem amazed, yet drawn, by this sharing which is so convincing.
>
> (Archbishop Flores of San Antonio, Texas, 'The Laity as Agents of Evangelization')

This involvement within the secular world can be a daunting task. It is very easy to retreat into the church community where one feels safe and secure. A strong sense of community, and involvement with like-minded people, a knowledge of being respected and valued, are the vitally attractive elements within our local churches. At the same time we must note that they can be the very things that prevent us from moving out into the wider world. Safe and secure, we want to remain within our own boundaries rather than move out into the insecure world around us. Faith and life cannot be divided, the one must affect the other. Our church life must influence our daily living.

> At the same time, these things have brought their own temptations. One is to become so caught up in church affairs as to fail in proper responsibility for the secular world. Another is to justify separating faith and life; to believe what the Gospel says rather than to live it out where one is.
>
> (*Christifideles Laici*, 2)

None of us, priests, pastors or lay people have the right to keep ourselves to ourselves. Furthermore, we do not have the right to keep the Gospel to ourselves. We cannot, we dare not, retreat into the safety of our churches believing that that is enough. We cannot, we dare not, create a dichotomy between professing our faith in our own communities and living out that faith in the wider world. If we do we are being untrue not only to the Gospel and to what the Church is all about, we are being untrue to ourselves.

So, the people of St Michael's must not only work to make their church a united one in which all have a part to play and all receive strength, they must also endeavour to equip people to live out their faith. St Michael's must become a 'power-house' in which people are able to gain understanding about how faith and life intertwine, and strength to put that faith into action.

Question: How is my faith related to the rest of my life, my family, my friends, the way I do my work, the way I get on with my fellow workers, my neighbours?

Question: What fears do I have about the relationship between my life of faith and my responsibility to live it out?

2. Living our faith

So far we have seen that the task of proclaiming the Gospel is a task for all. It is certainly not confined to the role of the priest, minister or church leader. We must turn now to thinking about how we are to do this. We sometimes express it in terms of sharing in the kingly, prophetic and priestly work of Christ. We need to unpack this a little to see what it means in everyday terms.

Sharing the kingly work of Christ

By baptism, every Christian shares in Christ's victory over all that works against us and stops us being with God. Christ is at one with God and wants us to share that closeness which he has with the Father. He has gone before us and conquered evil and death. That victory can be ours too. When William's son died in a car accident, all his father could think of was the injustice of a life cut short. Angry and confused, William blamed God for what had happened. Three years later he still does not understand but he can now say that his faith has carried him through and that somehow he was, and is, certain that death is not the end. He knows too that for him life will never be the same again but despite that, it is possible to make new beginnings. As William put it, 'The crucifixion of the last three years has become the dawn of a resurrection. In the midst of winter I have seen a glimpse of the spring I believe in. I know that Christ is stronger than death.' Sharing this victory of Christ applies as much to coping with life as coping with death. For many people today life seems to be a living death with no hope and no future. We do not have all the solutions nor can we even answer all the questions, but, in faith, we do have a way of starting to make some sense of what happens to us. We can know that we are not alone and that through our baptism Christ lives in us and we live in Christ, so his power to help us overcome all that keeps us from God is also available to us. We share in his kingship.

Sharing the teaching and prophetic work of Christ

Our baptism also makes us part of Christ in his teaching and prophetic work. Every Christian has the task of being a channel through which others can recognize God who is present within their lives. We share in that work of Christ to evangelize. As Pope Paul VI said: 'Jesus Christ, the Good News of God, was the very first and the greatest evangelizer' (*Evangelii Nuntiandi*, 7). His work is ours because we are part of him. So William, through his tragic loss, now shares that experience of despair, sorrow and bereavement with others, and, doing so, he shares the new hope and freedom which Christ offers.

Sharing the priestly work of Christ

Finally, our baptism enables us to share in the priestly work of Christ. We are called to consecrate our own lives so that others might know that fullness of life that Christ promised.

> More than a programme, evangelization is an attitude. It is a mentality of sharing, of inviting, of welcoming people into the joy of communion with Jesus Christ.
>
> (Texas Bishops, *Pastoral Letter on Evangelization*)

That mentality of sharing faith necessitates a giving of ourselves to the uttermost. It demands a consecration of our lives to God in the knowledge that in so doing we are opening ourselves to be used by him. It is indeed priestly work. When William shares his story with others he is opening himself to their gaze. He is putting himself on the line knowing that his experience may be misunderstood or rejected. It takes courage to talk of such a personal experience because there is always a risk involved; the risk of new pain and new crucifixion. Yet only by this sort of costly consecration can Christ's work be known.

This universal calling of Christians to share in Christ's mission finds expression in different ways. For some it will be the ordained ministry but for others there are different tasks to do and different work to be undertaken. What is important here is that all these different tasks and ministries work together. The Church is impoverished if that richness and variety is not present, or if all the work is left to one or two people. The Church needs all the different gifts that God has given to its members. It needs to experience the wealth of treasure that it has within those who make up the Body of Christ. It is when we recognize this that we are also capable of understanding that evangelization can take many different forms as people exercise the gifts they have. It is to this subject that we now turn.

Question: How do you share in the victory of Christ?

Question: How do you share in the teaching and prophetic work of Christ?

Question: In what practical ways is your commitment to Christ lived out in terms of costly consecration to him?

Group work on the theme:
The laity and evangelization

You may like to work on these ideas by using the following exercise.

Step 1
Begin by asking for the guidance of the Holy Spirit.

Step 2
Using the questions below, either alone or in pairs, think out how you see your role as a sharer in the mission of Christ.

1. CHRIST THE VICTOR AND KING: SHARING THE KINGSHIP OF CHRIST

In the light of William's story share:

(a) What kind of crucifixion do people you know face?

(b) What causes you anxiety and pain?

(c) What signs of victory and resurrection do you see?

2. CHRIST THE PROPHET/TEACHER: SHARING THE MISSION OF CHRIST

In the light of William's story and your answers to question 1: How do you share your experiences of Christ with you in your life with others?

3. CHRIST THE PRIEST: SHARING THE WORK OF CONSECRATION

In the light of William's story and your answers to question 2:

(a) What does sharing your faith cost?

(b) How committed are you to sharing your faith?

(c) In what way does your life 'consecrate' the world?

Step 3

Share in groups of six your discoveries — what, if anything, do you have in common?

What diversity do you see?

Step 4

In the whole group discuss what your findings have to say about the task of your local church (be specific).

Step 5

Commit your future to God asking him to use you and to work through you.

2. Discovering our gifts

Having seen the importance of the role of *all* Christ's people, clergy, religious and lay in the life and mission of the Church to proclaim Christ, we also need to recognize the talents of the people we have. Indeed we need to recognize our own gifts. It is a sad fact of life that very many local churches fail to recognize the ability and the gifts that lie locked up within their members. There lies a vast pool of uncovered and unused talent within our local churches. Not only do we hide it from one another, we very often hide it from ourselves.

It is therefore vital that we find ways of discovering the gifts that lie within our parish and that we match the gifts to the needs of the community around us. What follows is a suggested way of making those discoveries about the talents we have.

Group work on the theme: Discovering our gifts

This exercise is designed to help us discover the talents among us and see afresh the gifts we ourselves possess.

Step 1
Pray that God will lead you.

Step 2
In the group give each person a sheet of paper and a pen. Ask them to write their name at the top and, at the bottom of the sheet, one thing they think they are good at or one talent they possess. Fold the bottom over so that no one can see what has been written but leave plenty of room for more to be written above it.

Step 3
Pass the paper to the person on the right. This person writes down what gift or talent they see in the person named at the top of the paper and again the paper is folded upwards. This process continues around the circle until the paper returns to its original owner. (Stress the need for people to be honest and that no cheating is allowed!)

Step 4
Undo your paper and look at what others see in you.

Step 5
If you wish, make a list of the combined talents of the group.

Step 6
Spend some time together rejoicing in the gifts God has given you.

3. Using our gifts

Having discovered the gifts we have amongst us it is important
then that we use them well, properly and efficiently. Far too
often we simply muddle along hoping that people will use their
talents, and that somehow the gifts amongst us and the needs
that we have discovered will match themselves together. Unfortunately this does not always happen. So we get cases where
people are asked to do a particular task and feel neither com-
petent nor ready to undertake it. When this happens we are
surprised that people feel reticent about offering their services.
The truth of the matter is that people usually feel more comfortable if they are asked to do something they know they *can* do.
They are far more willing to do a task if they know that they
are likely to be happy doing it; that it is within their competence,
and that they are relatively good at it. In other words, we need
to make sure we put round pegs in round holes.

Square pegs in round holes

The result of this rather hit and miss attitude within the local
church is that we put square pegs in round holes. We get a
situation where a young man is asked to take on the task of
helping with the finances of the church and only reluctantly
does so knowing that this is not his major interest. His concern
is pastoral care. He is a good listener. He loves being with
people. Sitting next to him on a Sunday morning is a woman
who has given up her job as an accountant in order to bring
up her three children. She has all the relevant skills and she
has the interest and the ability. She finds it difficult to get out
in the evening because of the children but the financial work
necessary is something she could do at home. A little matching
of the gifts and the needs can do marvels. Here is a starter
which may help us think about this.

Group work on the theme:
Using our gifts

Step 1
Begin with a moment of silence.

Step 2
In the group use the facts you have discovered as a result of the work done in Chapter 4. What needs do you see as the most urgent? (Use your list of ten bad things and your reply on what you could do about them to help you in this.)

Step 3
Using your list of gifts discovered in the last exercise, see if you can 'match them up' with the needs you have now thought about.

Step 4
Discuss if there is anyone doing something with which they feel uncomfortable. Is there anyone not doing something they want to do and could do?

Step 5
What other gifts do you see in the members of your church which could be used to meet the needs? How are you going to help them to see their gifts and encourage them to use them?

Step 6
Make some *definite targets* or plans in the light of your findings.

Step 7
Close with a time of prayer committing your work to God.

Chapter 6

CALLED TO WITNESS
Telling the story, sharing the faith

1. Telling the story, sharing the faith — Answering questions

So far we have looked at the task of the local Christian community in evangelization in a number of different ways. We have looked at the necessity of entering into the real life of those around us and of responding to their real needs. In this chapter we shall think about how we, as individual Christians within our communities, can witness directly to our faith when the opportunity arises.

There is absolutely no doubt that the example of a life committed to Christ speaks volumes. What we do and how we live our lives is itself a means of evangelization. However, we must not allow ourselves to believe that this is *all* there is to evangelization. If we are living a truly Christian life and if that life is giving an example of Christlikeness then it is bound to raise questions for those with whom we come into contact. *Why* does this person I know act in this way? *What* value system does this person operate with? *Why* do they seem to have a dimension that I lack? *How* can they go on putting up with that irritating situation or person day after day? *Why* do they refuse to judge and hold in such high degree respect for others? Questions such as these and many others like them require answers. In reality we should be people for whom Jesus means so much that he is an inseparable part of us. He should be so much a part of us that it is impossible for others to understand *us* without reference to *him*. If therefore we are living a life filled with Christ, and these questions inevitably will arise if we are, then we must have some way of giving a reply to those who ask us. We must remember here that living the faith and telling the faith, proclamation by example and proclamation by word, are two sides of a single coin. We must resist the temptation to think that either of them is the only thing that matters as far as evangelization is concerned. Both are necessary. We need to share the faith both by what we are and by what we say.

We shall look here then at how we can equip ourselves to share faith and to answer those questions when people ask us. Some questions occur frequently and it is no bad thing to explore them together so that we are sure we have faced them and thought through what we believe about them. There are two parts to this exercise. The first is designed to help us develop skills of communication. The second is to help us answer questions.

Group work on the theme: Answering questions

Exercise 1

Step 1
Pray for God's guidance.

Step 2
Divide into pairs. One person speaks for one or two minutes about an important event of the past week.

The listener repeats the same story back to the speaker using his or her (the listener's) own words. The same ideas and events must be included, but the words are the listener's own.

After the listener has repeated the story, the speaker can correct anything that was not accurate.

Reverse roles and repeat the procedure.

Step 3
GOOD LISTENING
Think of the exercise you have just completed.

List on a flip-chart all the things that you can think of that:

• helped the process of speaking and listening;
• hindered the process of speaking or listening.

Step 4
ACCEPTING AND AFFIRMING
Choose another partner. One of the partners talks for one or two minutes about something he/she is proud of or good at.

When the speaker is finished, the listener makes a statement affirming, supporting, accepting or complimenting the speaker.

The speaker says how it felt to be affirmed. The listener says how if felt to do the affirming.

Switch roles and repeat the procedure. List in the whole group (no comments or discussion):

- What kind of responses are affirming?
- What kind are not affirming?

Discuss:

- Is it difficult or easy to be affirming?
- What helps? What hinders?

Step 5

MY VALUES; CAN I ACCEPT SOMEONE WHO DISAGREES?

Working alone, write down some statements that you cannot agree with. These could be religious belief statements, or opinions on moral issues. Incorrect factual statements will not work here. Some sample statements might be:

It is not Christian to get angry.

Christians are called to be involved in political issues.

The purpose of Christianity is to eradicate every other religion on earth.

Communism is a serious attempt to live the Gospel.

Heaven and hell exist on earth, now; there is no other place.

The Bible has a rule for every situation that can ever come up in human life.

Women should obey men.

Religion is an illusion which holds back the progress of humanity.

Young people should live together before they marry, try each other out.

Use these statements, or their opposites, or make up your own, but find statements that really oppose your values.

Try to remember someone you have spoken with who holds some of these views. If you can't remember anyone, imagine what such a person would say.

Think about these questions:

- How do you respond to that person?
- What would help you respond openly to that person?
- How can you express acceptance of that person without being dishonest about your own beliefs?

Share your thoughts with a partner.

Step 6

A BIBLICAL STORY: LISTENING AND ACCEPTING

Read Luke 15:11–32.

Discuss:
- How do you think the father felt when his younger son asked for his part of the inheritance?
- How did the father show that he listened to his son, accepted him, affirmed him?
- The father lost part of his property because he accepted his son's feelings, what did he gain?
- Do you think the father heard and accepted his older son as well?

During the session what new insights did you have?

Adapted from Anne Bishop and Eldon Hay, *Telling my Story, Sharing my Faith* (Division of Mission in Canada, The United Church of Canada).

Exercise 2

Step 1
Begin with a time of quiet.

Step 2
Sharing our faith will involve us at some point in trying to answer questions.

Here are some questions commonly asked by those enquiring about Christianity. Answer one of them now and try the others at regular intervals.

- How can God be a God of love when there's so much suffering in the world?
- Don't all religions lead to God?
- What about the heathen who have never heard the Good News?
- As long as you are sincere, does it matter what you believe?

- Can't I be a Christian without going to church?
- Isn't the Bible full of contradictions?
- What evidence is there for the Resurrection?
- Wasn't Jesus just a good man?
- Isn't death the end of everything?
- How can I know if I'm a Christian or not?
- Why are so many non-Christians nicer than Christians?

Try out your answers in the group.

Step 3
Here are some suggested 'helps' for you to discuss.

Don't be afraid of saying, 'I don't know, but what I do know is . . .' or, 'I will find out for you'.

Avoid fruitless argument (not *all* argument).

Spot the red herrings. Few people today have any informed knowledge about Christianity.

Sincerity is more valuable than 'proof'.

Remember that some people ask questions but don't really want an answer.

Take into account the whole person when answering their questions; their real need may be something completely different.

It is possible to win your argument but lose your listener. 'Winning' is not the objective.

Use language people can understand.

Step 4
Add other things that are important to remember in answering people's questions.

Step 5
Read 1 Peter 3:15. Pray for courage and strength.

Adapted from Gordon and Graham Jones, *What I've Always Wanted to Say* . . . (Church Pastoral Aid Society).

2. Telling the story — Sharing the faith

Lack of confidence

One of the greatest difficulties we experience with regard to sharing faith is a lack of confidence.

There was a man called Joe who worked in a factory as an engineer. He was also a keen member of his local church. The men at work constantly teased him about his membership of the church.

One day, however, one of the men took him aside and said, 'Joe, I know that I have frequently joked about the fact that you go to church, but I have been doing a great deal of thinking just lately and I want you to tell me why you are a Christian.'

Joe went to his minister that night and said, 'I felt so ashamed. I couldn't tell him.'

In some ways this feeling of inability to share faith can be a help rather than a hindrance because it ensures that we are more likely to be sensitive to the feelings of others. Rather than blundering in full of self-righteous zeal, our awareness of our own inadequacies acts as a safeguard. However, this lack of confidence can also be a real problem. It can be an excuse we use to opt out completely or it can so hamper us that we end up with a definite lack of enthusiasm for the whole enterprise. Confidence in the Gospel we proclaim and in the God whose Good News it is, is a necessity and so is confidence in ourselves.

This need for confidence should not lead us into riding rough-shod over others or in engaging in forms of evangelization which do more harm than good, but it should enable us sensitively to share our faith with others as and when it is right to do so.

The reasons for this lack of self-confidence are many and varied. We may be afraid that others will think us odd or religious fanatics. For instance, Mary Roper missed a golden opportunity to 'tell the story, share the faith', when her next door neighbour came round for coffee and began talking about her seven-year-old son's RE lesson at school. Mary, quite rightly, let Elaine talk about the difficulties she was finding in answering the child's questions but, when asked what she thought, Mary changed the subject as quickly as possible for fear that Elaine would think her a religious eccentric. What Mary failed to see was that Elaine had come round especially because each Sunday she saw the Roper family going to church. It had seemed to Elaine reasonable to suppose that they could help her out.

We may lack confidence because we are embarrassed when it comes to talking about God. This is quite understandable — after all, our relationship with God is a very private and personal affair and we assume that the relationship that other people have is equally special and should not be exposed too often. Naturally, sensitivity is the essential requirement here but, if we are asked about our religious beliefs, or more especially, if we are asked to share something of our own experience of God, we should try to do this with an openness which conveys to the other person that any relationship with God is a completely natural and normal thing to have.

Another reason for our lack of confidence is a fear of saying the wrong thing or of treading on dangerous ground. This fear is based on a well-founded awareness that we could do far more harm than good which is why sensitivity to the needs and feelings of others is, as always, so important. However, if our unwillingness is based on fear that others will ask us questions we will not be able to answer, the fear is more about not wanting to admit failure in knowledge than sensitivity to others. It is really an example of pride. For instance, take Peter, who refused ever to talk about religion. Deep down he knew that his refusal had very little to do with what others were thinking about God but everything to do with how they would react to him if he showed that he could not answer the questions which they had asked. Let us then look at our fears a little more closely.

Possible group work on the theme:
Lack of confidence

Step 1
Pray for openness and honesty to face the fears we have.

Step 2
Read 1 Peter 2:9–10.

Step 3
God calls us to live and speak and to 'declare the wonderful deeds' he has done. We are often afraid to do this.

Here is a shield.

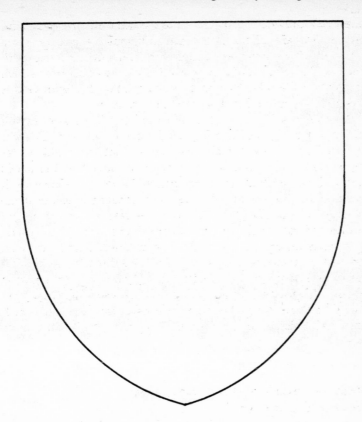

Write (or draw) what shield you use to hide behind when it comes to telling the story, sharing the faith.

Step 4
Share your 'shields' with each other.

Step 5
Talk about what would help you lay down your shield.

Step 6
What will you do about what you have discovered?

Step 7
Close with prayer.

Telling the story, Sharing the faith — With our friends

It is unfortunately true that all these fears are present not only in our dealings with those outside our communities but inside as well. We do not 'tell the story and share the faith' with those who share the same basic understanding as ourselves, let alone with those whose views are so very different. Often we are afraid of sharing it within our own small group. How difficult did you find it to share, even with your group, your answers to the questions in Section 1?

St Joseph's had a series of evening meetings in order to allow people to share their own experiences of faith with one another. At the initial meeting Michael found himself in a group of four people. They had been asked simply to talk in whatever way they wished about being on the Christian pilgrimage. They all found this quite difficult but Michael in particular found the whole experience quite disturbing. Talking to him afterwards I discovered that this was a combination of fear that his relationship with God was totally different from everybody else's (which of course it was not), and the very real difficulty of finding the right words to use in order to describe that experience. As the series of meetings progressed, his confidence grew as did his ability to find ways of expressing his faith in a natural and realistic way.

We need to have good experiences of telling the story, sharing the faith in the safety of our own group. If we can do this then we will find that we will be able to share faith with others in a way which is both natural to us and sensitive to them.

Group work on the theme:
Sharing the faith — With our friends

Step 1
Ask God to help you.

Step 2
Divide the group into pairs. The first person will speak for one minute on 'What my faith means to me'. (The listener must *not* interrupt.)

The second person 'plays back' or paraphrases what has been said.

Reverse the roles.

Step 3
In the group list:
- What was hard about speaking?
- What was hard about listening?

Step 4
Read Luke 24:13–27. What does the passage say about listening and speaking?

Step 5
Commit yourselves to God in a time of silence.

3. Telling the story, Sharing the faith — Ways forward

The process of telling the story and sharing the faith is going to be as different as the people with whom we come into contact. We have already noted the need to find ways which are natural to ourselves and the following exercises are designed to give us confidence in order to do just that. They should be undertaken within a small group with whom you feel comfortable and in whose security you trust.

Group work on the theme:
Ways forward

Exercise 1

Step 1
Pray.

Step 2

TELLING MY STORY: THE PEOPLE I TOUCH

List all the people you were in touch with this past week. Don't forget shop assistants, telephone operators, garage attendants as well as friends and family! Add up the number of people on your list.

As a total group, add up the number of people you came in contact with over the past week. Are you surprised at the number?

Step 3

HOW DID JESUS SHARE HIS MESSAGE?

Jesus shared his message in a variety of ways and in a variety of situations.

List the different ways that Jesus shared his message — as many as you can think of.

Give each person one (or more) of the following Scripture passages. Have them read the passage(s) and write down the method that Jesus used to share his message:

Matthew 5:1, 2   Matthew 21:12, 13
Mark 14:32–34   John 1:37–39
Luke 4:33–37   Matthew 23:13–15
Mark 4:33   John 2:1, 2
Matthew 19:13–15   Matthew 9:10–11
John 3:1–6   Matthew 4:24

If any of these are not on your list, add them.

Step 4

HOW DO I COMMUNICATE MY FAITH?

Individually, list the different ways you communicate your faith.

Look again at the list of people you were in touch with this week.
● How did you show your faith to them?
● How could you share more of your faith with them?

Would any of them especially appreciate or benefit from an expression of your faith in word or action? Who? What would be an appropriate way to express your faith to them?

Share whatever you wish with one other person.

Adapted from Anne Bishop and Eldon Hay, *Telling my Story, Sharing my Faith* (Division of Mission in Canada, The United Church of Canada).

Exercise 2

Step 1
Pray for the guidance of the Holy Spirit.

Working alone, think about a significant event in your life. Tell it to *one* member of the group. Choose a story that was a turning point for you. Tell it as it happened.

Step 2

MY STORY: PART OF GOD'S STORY

On the next page you will find the outline of a chart. Write the main points of your story in the left-hand column, and then move across filling in whatever comes into your head in the other columns. Be light and flexible with this exercise. Put things down even if they seem ridiculous, and if nothing comes under a certain heading, just leave it blank. An example is given at the top of the chart.

Step 3

Tell the story to your partner again. This time try to tell it as a story of the action of God in your life. Did God get a message through to you? Tell you that he loves you? Direct your course? Surprise you? Call you? Correct you? Perhaps you told the story this way the first time. In that case, expand on it, tell more.

Step 4

With your partner answer these questions:

- What was the difference in the two stories?
- Which story did you like telling best? Why?
- Which did the listener like best? Why?
- In what situations would you tell the first version of the story?
- In what situations would you tell the second version?

Step 5

Thank God that your story is part of God's action in your life.

Adapted from Anne Bishop and Eldon Hay, *Telling my Story, Sharing my Faith* (Division of Mission in Canada, The United Church of Canada).

Significant event	Feelings	Song, symbol, quotation	Bible verses, stories, themes
Wanted to get off the farm but couldn't get a job in town.	Restless, desperate to get away, discouraged, hopeless.		'The stone the builders rejected has become the cornerstone.'
The Peters asked me to paint their barn.		'When God closes a door, he always opens a window.'	My parents looked down on the Peters because they didn't speak good English. Working for them, I thought, was as low as I could get — and then Mrs P. changed my life.
Mrs Peters asked why I looked so unhappy all the time.	Surprise — someone noticed!		
Told her all about it.			'If you have ears to hear, then hear.'
She listened, urged me to go on and study at the college.	Relief — someone cared!		I was trying so hard to get off the farm in one way (a job), that I couldn't hear God calling me for something else. I had to give up all hope before I heard him!
I did, always went back to her whenever I needed to talk.	Strength — someone believed in me!		

Now try it with your story:

Significant event	Feelings	A folk song, symbol, hymn, poem, or quotation which comes to mind	Bible verses, stories, themes, images which come to mind

Exercise 3

Step 1

You see the following advertisement in your community or church paper.

WANTED: EVANGELIST

Wanted immediately: evangelist in this community. Must be committed and willing to become better on the job. Person can work at home or in present occupation. Please apply in writing using the following guidelines:

My experience in story-telling/faith expression.
My strengths as a person and evangelist.
Areas where I want to grow and improve.
Why I see evangelization as important.

Send applications to God, care of this newspaper.

Step 2

Apply for the job.

Step 3

Share with the whole group.

Adapted from Anne Bishop and Eldon Hay, *Telling my Story, Sharing my Faith* (Division of Mission in Canada, The United Church of Canada).

Chapter 7

CALLED TO EXPLORE
Further suggestions for group work

We have given many different examples and offered many exercises in this book which have been designed to help you think through your own situation.

This chapter contains a collection of further group and/or individual activities which may be helpful. Be selective about which ones you use. They will not all be suitable or useful and, above all, adapt the material for your own group. It is important to tailor the sessions so that they are right for the people you are with. There is no blueprint for group work anymore than the book is a blueprint for evangelization. Think of it as a supermarket and pick off the shelf what seems right. Then, once you have made your choice, use the product as and how you wish.

Aware of Christ

Step 1
Choose a leader (2 minutes).

Step 2
For three minutes think quietly about your day today. Thank God for his presence.

Step 3
Write down briefly where today you were aware of Christ's presence with you (5 minutes).

Step 4
Each member of the group share something of what has been written down (as much as each one wishes). (15 minutes.)

Step 5
Note down the areas of life most often occurring in this discussion. (5 minutes.)

Step 6
What does this say to us about the faith we have to express? (10 minutes.)

Questions — But no answers

Common questions which are asked by Christians as well as non-Christians can be the basis of many ways of sharing the faith. But we need to work through such questions ourselves. How would *you* answer the following?

- Why does God allow evil?
- I can be good without being a Christian, so why be one?
- Why does Christianity think it has elements of the truth which are not a part of other faiths?
- Why is the Bible so important?
- Why do I have to go to church to be a Christian?
- How can Christians say God is the source of unity when they hate and kill each other?
- How can Christians believe in the Bible when science has disproved it?
- How can you know there is a heaven?
- What happens to us when we die?

You might like to share what each of you would say and gently discuss your answers. Be careful. Do not destroy people's confidence or make anyone feel a failure as you do this.

Using the right language

One of the difficulties we face when sharing faith is that of the words we use. It is very easy to fall into religious jargon which, though it may mean a lot to us, does not communicate to others. Sometimes, too, we do not really understand this language ourselves. To help us explore our faith more deeply and to help us in our conversations with others try putting the following into 'non-religious' language.

Jesus is the image of the Father.
Jesus is the Incarnate Son of God.
Jesus died for our sins.
Jesus ascended into heaven.
God is three persons in one.

You might like to do this on your own at home and later share (sensitively!) in the group.

Discuss, too, what you have learned from this exercise.

Tasks for Christians

Step 1
Have some large sheets of paper ready and thick felt pens.

Step 2
Ask the group to produce a joint list of 'tasks for Christians'.

Do not reject any suggestion as 'wrong' (within reason!). *Do not* discuss — just list. Keep going until you have a good selection of tasks.

Step 3
Now make a list of what *actually* happens in your church. *Be honest* — do not wear rose-tinted spectacles.

Step 4
In your community what tasks are you:
(a) good at
(b) not bad at
(c) poor at
(d) not doing at all?

Step 5
What conclusions do you draw from this?

My Gospel (individual exercise)

Step 1
Paul speaks of 'my Gospel' in 2 Timothy 2:8. What is *your* Gospel? (Avoid technical words and jargon.) What is the Good News for you?

Step 2
Think of someone you know who does not profess to be a Christian. Would any of your Good News be Good News for them? What? Why?

Step 3
Spend a moment thanking God for the Good News you have. Pray for the person you have thought about and thank God for what they have shown you.

Recommendations

Look at the following recommendations from a small group working on the theme of evangelization. They recommended that their church should:
(a) Put mission at the top of the agenda.
(b) Undertake an assessment of the needs of the area.
(c) Equip people for the task by developing their gifts and giving confidence.
(d) Develop strategies to meet the needs which arise from the assessment.

If you had such a group in your church what would you want to add, alter or take away from these recommendations?

Deepest needs

Here are three statements from people about their aim in life.

'My aim in life is to treat others as I would like them to treat me.'

'My aim in life is to look out for myself and have enough money to do what I want to do.'

'My aim in life is to keep my family well-fed, clothed and happy, even if I have to nearly kill myself to do it.'

Discuss:
● Do you agree with any of these aims?
● What other aims do people *you know* have?
● What is your aim in life?
● Have your aims changed?

Read Mark 6:30–44:
● What were the needs of the crowd?
● What were the needs of the disciples?
● What needs did Jesus see?

If you can, discuss (sensitively and without pressing people): How Christ meets your deepest needs.

From outer space

You will need: a large selection of local newspapers, magazines and church papers. The group needs to use about ten varied documents. They need not be new.

Step 1
Let the group imagine they are visitors from outer space. The group is given the ten assorted documents. Assuming no language barriers, study the papers to find answers to the following questions (which need to be duplicated in advance for each participant). Findings should be listed.

OUR CULTURE — A PROBE

  i What seem to be the main interests of people?
  ii How do they spend their time?
  iii To what ends does society appear to commit itself?
  iv What do the advertisements suggest about what people want?
  v What do Mr and Mrs Average expect to get out of life?
  vi If visitors from outer space were 'religious' what might they discern about our religion?
  vii What appear to be the ways in which our moral traditions are passed on to succeeding generations?
  viii Is the overall impression one of satisfaction, boredom or hysteria or what?

Step 2
In the light of your work what conclusions do you draw about our society?

Step 3
What does the Gospel have to say about your conclusion?

Evaluation

If you are running a course of sessions to explore the theme of evangelization, you may wish to use an evaluation sheet. This is always a useful check on what is happening in the group. You could use it in the middle (to give you a chance to make changes) and at the end.

EVALUATION SHEET

1. What do you feel about the meeting? Express your feelings by putting a tick on this list:

☐ Very unsatisfactory
☐ Rather unsatisfactory
☐ Neutral
☐ Satisfactory
☐ Very satisfactory.

2. Say, if you like, why you feel this way.
3. What has been most helpful (so far)?
4. What has been unhelpful (so far)?
5. Have you any other difficulties, problems or hopes which you would like future meetings to take into account?
6. Any other comments?

Evangelization checklist

1. Do you see God as the primary agent of evangelization?
Does our approach show that it is God's power and not simply our techniques which is transforming and saving the world? Are prayer, good liturgy and personal renewal central to our evangelizing activity?

2. Do we see evangelization as everyone's responsibility?
Do we see the responsibility for evangelization being mainly with priests and Sisters, or is it something for each and every member of the Church? What are we doing to give people the understanding and skills to carry it out?

3. Do we communicate God's love?
Do people experience us as warm, cheerful and compassionate? Does the example of our lives communicate the experience of God's love? Are we willing to share our faith in words as well as deeds?

4. Is total human betterment part of our mission?
Do we understand the link between evangelization and liberation? What have we done to improve the social condition of those we minister to? In what ways have we set people free from poverty, hunger, discrimination, disease, unemployment and inadequate housing?

5. Do we respect other traditions?

Do we affirm people's basic goodness and value as created by God and seek to learn from their moral insights rather than assume they are godless and devoid of truth? Do we judge them by our own standards or do we try to understand theirs? Do we respect their cultural heritage?

6. Does our love go beyond our borders?

Is the church community truly concerned about every person in our area and not only the Christians?

7. Is our approach ecumenical?

Have we taken the time to discover and celebrate what we share in common with other Churches? In what ways have we undertaken common and co-operative ecumenical ventures?

8. Do we use modern media?

How have we used modern methods of communication? Are we making effective use of the printed word and local radio and television?

9. Do we fully use existing groups?

Have we explored and affirmed the strengths of existing parish organizations and considered how their evangelizing roles can be intensified?

10. What is our total image?

What do we as individuals or as a local community communicate to the unchurched? What do we communicate in terms of activities on behalf of justice, our lifestyles, our presence in the community? How inviting is our church to the unchurched in everything it says and does?

These notes are adapted from a report to the Diocese of Cincinnati and used in England and Wales by the Office for Evangelization.